A CHANGING AMERICA

CONSERVATIVES VIEW THE '80s FROM THE UNITED STATES SENATE

BY

Senator Pete Domenici
Senator Jake Garn
Senator Orrin Hatch
Senator Paul Laxalt
Senator James McClure
Senator Richard Schweiker
Senator Malcolm Wallop

edited by
Senator Paul Laxalt and
Richard S. Williamson

REGNERY/GATEWAY, INC.   South Bend, Indiana

CONTENTS

FOREWORD

By HONORABLE RONALD REAGAN

Someone once said that the difference between an American and any other kind of person is that an American lives *in anticipation* of the future, because he knows it will be great. Other people *fear* the future as just a repetition of past failures. There's a lot of truth in that. If there is one thing we are sure of, it is that history need not be relived; that nothing is impossible, and that man *is* capable of improving his circumstances.

I am hopeful for America in the 1980s. I have faith that they will be years of new prosperity and strength.

Today America does face serious problems. Double digit inflation has robbed us and our families of the ability to plan. It has destroyed the confidence to buy, and it threatens the very structure of family life itself as more and more wives are forced to work in order to help meet the ever increasing cost of living. At the same time, the lack of real growth in the economy has introduced the justifiable fear in the minds of working men and women, who are already overextended, that soon there will be fewer jobs and no money to pay for even the necessities of life.

Another serious problem is our energy situation. Today, energy is no longer cheap, and we face the prospect that some forms of energy soon may not be available at all.

And in the foreign arena, the United States and its allies face severe pressures as we enter the 1980s. The crisis in Iran and the Soviet invasion of Afghanistan are the latest tests of our resolve and our commitment. We must judge carefully. Though we should leave no initiative unturned in our pursuit of peace, we must be clear voiced in our resolve to resist unpeaceful acts.

Too often in recent times, we have just drifted along with world events, responding as if we thought of ourselves as a nation in decline. To our allies, we seem to appear to be a nation unable to make decisions in its own interest, let alone in the common interest. It is foolhardy not to have a long-range diplomatic strategy of our own. The world has become a place where, in order to survive, our country needs more than just allies—it needs real friends. Yet in recent times we often seem not to have recognized who our friends are.

These problems are not the result of any failure of the American spirit, they are a failure of our leaders to establish rational goals and give our people something to order their lives by.

I believe the United States needs to set a new agenda. The leadership must be strong, active, and with clear vision. And I believe the American people *want* that new agenda, and are ready for strong leadership.

Therefore, I was pleased when my good friend Paul Laxalt told me about this book and asked me to write an introduction. Paul and I have been friends for many years. While I was governor of California, Paul was governor of neighboring Nevada. Since Paul went to the Senate in 1974 we have continued to work together both politically and on important issues.

Senator Paul Laxalt and the six other distinguished senators who have written chapters for this book have provided a valuable service. Each senator has written his own analysis of an important issue area and presented positive, forward-looking proposals to address our problems and to expand America's horizons in the 1980s.

While each senator has spoken only for himself, there is a common theme. These men, like myself, have faith in the American spirit. Each wants to get the government roadblocks out of the way to unleash the energy and talent of the American people.

I believe this nation hungers for a spiritual revival; hungers to once again see honor placed above political expediency; to see government once again the protector of our liberties, not the distributor of gifts and privilege. Government should uphold—and not undermine—those institutions which are custodians of the very values upon which civilization is founded: religion, education and, above all, family. Government cannot be clergyman, teacher, and parent. It is our servant, beholden to us.

In this book, seven of my friends, each a talented leader in his own right, draw upon their insight and experience in the United States Senate, to present their views on how to meet the problems of the '80s. It is an important contribution to the public debate through which we will set a new agenda for the United States.

ACKNOWLEDGMENTS

The contributors to this book wish to thank the many people who helped us with this project. Without their contributions of time and talent, this book would not have been written. We wish particularly to thank the following people: Penny Eastman, John Laxalt, Al Drischler, Rick Spees, Steve Bell, Ty McCoy, Jeff Bingham, Bob Hunter, Mike Morgan, Mike Hathaway, General Dan Graham, Ed Meese, and Dave Winston.

ACKNOWLEDGMENTS

COMMENTARY

By SENATOR PAUL LAXALT

We must enter the 1980s with a clear realization of the challenges and opportunities facing us.

On the foreign front, our formidable problems have, justifiably, dominated our thoughts, our conversations, and our media coverage for many months. Iran and the Soviet Union have chosen to bring into question before the world our courage and resolve, and our once "sacred" dollar continues to be irreverently battered by the international financial community.

Domestically, every man, woman, and child has been touched by the twin plagues of rising prices and declining energy. Our rate of inflation has risen in three years from 4.8% to 13.4%, and the solution to our energy problem remains to be found.

Against this backdrop of momentous and highly visible issues, there exists still another problem area—equally momentous, but much less visible. I speak of the growing threats to our traditional values and institutions and the resulting assault upon the American spirit. I speak of the American family.

Under attack though it is, the American family must survive. I firmly believe that, if the family is destroyed, our society as we know it will follow. It is imperative, therefore, that we become aware of this serious problem and examine means of preserving and protecting this basic unit of our society.

Let me state at the outset, however, that despite the present atmosphere *I am optimistic* about the fate of the American spirit and family. I have faith in the American Dream, and I intend to do everything in my limited power to make sure it continues to be an achievable goal.

My optimism is based principally upon my own family background. My parents were French Basque immigrants who came, like millions of others, in search of the American Dream. They settled in Nevada.

My father was a sheepherder, an occupation which kept him in the Sierra Nevada mountains for long periods of time.

My mother, a deeply religious woman, in addition to raising six children, ran a small boarding hotel in Carson City. Having been trained at Cordon Bleu in Paris, her food was well known and appreciated throughout the area. In raising us she ran a "tight ship," even oppressive by some modern day standards. When she made a family decision, that was it. No appeal. No due process. And yet, we all survived, for we knew she had our interests at heart.

Through sheer hard work and extreme financial sacrifice my parents realized that dream. They raised and educated six children—two girls and four boys.

They raised us with deep values. We were taught utmost respect for our institutions: the family, school, church—and, yes, public officials.

One daughter is a Catholic nun, the other a teacher with a family of her own. One son became a writer and historian. Three sons are attorneys, one of whom strayed into politics.

This all was accomplished in an atmosphere of self-reliance and independence. We were taught early to take care of ourselves, that to rely upon others, particularly government, would quickly result in unwanted restrictions of our personal liberties and lessening of our self-esteem.

These are my roots, and they have served as the foundation for my political philosophy throughout my public life.

During the '60s and '70s, there were times when I was greatly concerned about what was happening to our sense of traditional values in this country. But as I mentioned before, I am now optimistic about the 1980s. I feel we will witness a reassertion of the traditional institutions which have served us so well in the past, and in the process we will see a *diminished role* for the federal government, particularly insofar as the family is concerned.

If we accept the premise that the family is the very foundation upon which our nation and society is structured, then I believe we have the obligation to protect it from those in the federal government who, wittingly or otherwise, persist in meddling and tampering with this most sacred institution.

The early pilgrims came over here partly in order to raise their children in their own religious ways and not according to the English state-dictated church edicts. Their determination to be free and independent resulted in the family farm, upon which our young nation was largely dependent for survival and wealth. As our nation grew and became independent, our democratic institutions built upon and, at the same time, enhanced our families. Alex de Tocqueville described it quite well in 1834 in his *Democracy in America:*

As long as family spirit endured a man fighting against tyranny was never alone, for he had around him clients, hereditary friends and relations. And even were this support lacking, he would still have felt sustained by his ancestors and by his descendants.

Later, for millions of immigrants entering this country, the family provided their only fixed source of support. *Without government assistance or interference,* these people cared for each other, provided for each other, educated their young, and in the process built the world's most advanced civilization and highest standard of living.

I think President William McKinley may have put it best when he said:

The American home constitutes the strength, security, and integrity of our government . . . it is the foundation of a pure national life. The good home makes the good citizen . . . good government necessarily follows.

Yet despite these acknowledged benefits, the family has come under assault. Economic and social pressures attributed to economic growth, urbanization, and the rise of large economic units have all served to fragment families and focus production and consumption on the individual, at the expense of the family. These are serious concerns, but even more devastating has been the impact of federal government policies.

Starting in the 1930s and accelerating during the last twenty years, the federal government has taken upon itself to become involved in American life in a multitude of ways. And as I see it, this involvement has frequently been disruptive.

Let me cite a few brief examples. The tax code encourages two working people to live together rather than marry. The Medicaid program provides fuller coverage for elderly relatives living in an institution rather than with their families. Aid to families with dependent children (AFDC) is structured to encourage fathers of poor families to leave home. Federal programs for education have created a monolithic, educational bureaucracy that looks on parents with distrust, and disrupts the traditional parent-school board relationship. There is even a proposal of HEW to create a Children's Bill of Rights which would allow courts to examine the most intimate of parent-child relations. These are but a few examples of government programs that have intruded on every facet of family life.

The impact of these programs, despite their good intentions, has been to seriously harm the family. Divorce rates, one-parent families, and juvenile crime rates have reached historically high levels. Family members are separated and estranged from each other as the government usurps family roles. Solid family relationships have been replaced by an intrusive bureaucratic presence.

Despite these undesirable developments, I believe we are *turning the corner* toward a more stable family life in America. We Americans are a practical people. We are skeptical of abstractions, and we tend to put our basic trust in real world, practical experience. The theories of liberalism of the 1960s have, if anything, reinforced that fundamental pragmatism. It has become clear that the state is not an acceptable substitute for the child-rearing, educational, health care, and housing functions traditionally performed in American society by the family.

I sense this fundamental change in societal attitudes. I believe that people are perceiving the basic hollowness of a society in which the role of the family is minimized. I believe our people are returning to the traditional family principles and values which have made us the great nation we are.

In addition, I can see a gradual change taking place in governmental policies and legislation. Attempts are being made through reform or repeal of existing programs to *remove* the disincentives to family life currently on the books. On the other hand, and more positively, incentives —primarily through the tax code—are being implemented to encourage the growth and flowering of the American family. Encouraging as these initial steps are, however, I am convinced that only a sustained effort in the years ahead will totally restore the family to its proper place of respect in our society.

On balance, then, I am confident that, building upon our traditional values and institutions, primarily the family, we will see the 1980s as a decade of renewed growth and prosperity at home and new strength and leadership among the nations of the world.

My confidence is shared by many of the leaders of the next decade, some of whom speak for themselves in this volume, including Pete Domenici on the economy, Jake Garn on defense, Orrin Hatch on labor relations, Jim McClure on energy, Dick Schweiker on health, and Malcolm Wallop on the environment. These men are the bright, emerging stars of the next decade, and I am pleased and honored to be associated with them in this effort.

The 1980s can indeed be a time of vigor and expanding horizons. They can be an exciting time, calling for the best efforts of our nation to achieve even higher levels of greatness. This is a vision I share with my good friends and coauthors. But each of us realizes full well that the integrity of our traditional institutions *needs to be preserved* through sound governmental policies, domestic and foreign. That's what this book is all about.

BUDGET & ECONOMY
RESTORING PRIVATE INITIATIVE

By SENATOR PETE DOMENICI

Late in 1979, opinion polls showed a disturbing trend in the thinking of Americans: large numbers of Americans were feeling insecure about the future of the nation. Too many of them felt "helpless," and believed that severe economic times lay immediately ahead.

As the father of eight children, three of them in college, I fully understand this sense of helplessness. That's exactly the way my wife Nancy and I feel when we go shopping to try to make the family budget balance at the end of the month. Economically, Americans find themselves much like Alice in Wonderland, who had to run as fast as she could just to stay even.

This irony—that the richest nation on earth should be fearful of economic bad times—might be amusing, except for the fact that the problems in our economy which Americans are intuitively becoming aware of are *real*. Our free enterprise system, beset by inflation and persistently high unemployment, is in danger.

I contend that strains within our free enterprise economy are directly related to the new relationship between the private sector (business and individuals at work) and the public sector (government in all its forms). The public sector has grown to such gigantic proportions that more than one-third of the nation's Gross National

1

Product was taken in taxes by government at all levels in 1979. Even this was not enough to satisfy the needs of government. The federal deficit continues to soar. As government voraciously continues to expand, our private sector weakens; we have fewer goods and services for our people; and we begin to lose the vitality given to America by an individual-oriented, incentive-based economy.

But what is even more ominous, we have begun to lose personal freedom. The right to pursue one's own material goals cannot be separated from personal freedom. And as government has grown, so has the personal freedom of Americans increasingly come under attack.

My friend Don Brewer, of Artesia, New Mexico, symbolizes the kind of hard-working American who ought to be rewarded by "the system," but who not too long ago found himself a victim of the system instead. The owner of a small oil distributing company, Don had worked long hours to make a go of it in Southeastern New Mexico. As the government began to intrude more and more into the energy business in the mid-1970s, Don found himself set upon by bureaucrats from the Federal Energy Administration. Despite his best efforts, and despite the fact that he was running a one-man show, Don had violated some extremely complicated pricing regulations, the bureacrats alleged. A lengthy legal battle ensued, and Don faced virtual bankruptcy—even though the evidence he eventually presented to me, in his desperate last-ditch attempt to save himself, showed that whatever violations had occurred were minor and inadvertent. Only after our office intervened with the agency on Don's behalf did we manage to persuade the bureaucrats that they had been barking up the wrong tree. But two years of harassment and expense meant that Don had to start all over again to rebuild his business and his reputation. His personal freedom, tied up with his economic freedom, had suffered.

The free enterprise system that has served this nation so well is still vibrant, and can still meet our needs better than any other system devised by man. But it can also be destroyed. To make sure that our children, and their children, have the same high quality of life we enjoy, and that they have this quality of life with the same personal freedom that Americans have also held dear, we need to restore the energy of our free enterprise system. In the following pages, I analyze the excessive government intervention in our economy and the basic flaws in the way our federal government conducts its own budgetary business. Then I present an agenda of positive proposals for economic prosperity for the 1980s.

At stake is nothing less than the freedom Americans have sacrificed so many lives to maintain. To lose this precious freedom to the *insidious and silent growth of government* would be one of the greatest tragedies in history.

It was clear-eyed Will Rogers who spotted the fundamental change The Great Depression brought about in America. He observed that Franklin Roosevelt's idea of government was "a milk cow with a thousand teats." But Will's placid milk cow has been transformed, by 40 years of rampant growth, into a monster with a thousand *mouths.* In an attempt to satisfy the rising expectations fueled by political rhetoric and a period of unprecented economic prosperity, this government monster must have more and more food in the form of our tax dollars.

Statistics tell part of the story. In 1930, taxes of all

3

sorts accounted for about 15 percent of all personal income. Today, taxes take about 40 percent of it. Americans work until mid-May just to earn enough money to pay local, state, and federal taxes! Only as the spring fades do we get to work for ourselves and our families, instead of for the government. As for the size of the federal budget, it has leaped from less than $100 billion in 1961 to *more than $530 billion* for fiscal year 1980.

And as government has grown, a revolution has occurred in its functions. Purchasing goods and services no longer stands as its primary task; the United States now spends more money through programs designed to *redistribute* wealth than it spends to buy goods and services. *Handling transfer payments and grants* to other government entities emerged, in 1971, as our government's main preoccupation—a clear change from the earlier, traditional role of government.

The interest on America's national debt dramatizes the extent of our wasteful spending habits and backward priorities. So enormous is our national debt now that *gross interest* on it, for fiscal year 1980, will be nearly $66 billion (the size of the entire federal budget in 1952 —during the Korean War).

An insight into the size of the federal budget comes when you realize how we on the Senate Budget Committee handle these incredibly large numbers. We drop all the zeros. Thus, $100,000,000 (an enormous number to most of us) becomes simply .1; $50,000,000 becomes .05 Such insignificant sums as $1,500,000 aren't even noted. The air of unreality such numerical shorthand brings to the budget process may contribute to the failure of Congress to discipline spending. After all, it's hard to get very upset when one of your colleagues says, "Oh, let's just add .3 to that spending area." It's only after you realize that .3 is really $300,000,000 in tax dollars—the total yearly earnings of more than 20,000 average American families—that you're brought back to a recognition of what you are doing.

I recall most vividly one exchange between senators and members of the House of Representatives during a heated conference to reach final spending numbers of the federal government's 1980 budget. After nine days of solid negotiations, we on the Senate offered to add more than $500 million in spending for social programs, even though we had real evidence that the social programs in question had plenty of carry-over funds, and didn't need the money. The House conferees were aghast. They argued for more. Eventually, Senator Muskie, chairman of the Senate Budget Committee, exclaimed in exasperation, "I think our constituents would find it absurd that we are fighting about sums this small in a budget this big!" Actually, I suspect that our constituents would find it *refreshing* that we fight about half a billion dollars, and would be dismayed if we failed to. (As a lamentable footnote, I should point out that the House won most of the battles that day and, as a result, social program spending for 1980 soared about $1 billion higher than it should have.)

Like a snowball rolling down a hill, the rate of growth of the federal budget has increased, and gained constantly in momentum, in recent years. During the 1950s and 1960s, federal spending grew at an annual rate of about 2.8 percent. In the 1970s, the growth rate averaged 8.6 percent—with a 9.9 percent growth rate in 1977 and an 11.9 percent rate in 1978.

Early in 1979, President Jimmy Carter announced that he would embark on a "lean and austere" fiscal plan for 1980. Those were his words, much bandied-about in the nation's headlines. Predictably, when the calculations were all in, the "lean and austere" budget showed an increase of 9.7 percent over 1979 fiscal year spending. All of the gains that the Senate Budget Committee had made in its first recommendations on spending levels for 1980 had been lost: spending had gone from a 7.6 percent gain (below the projected 1980 rate of inflation) to a 9.7 percent increase over 1979 levels (above the projected rate of inflation for 1980). The monster had grown again.

As a long-time "monster fighter," I found the failure of the budget process in 1979 especially disheartening. This failure came after the most enlightening hearings in the Senate Budget Committee's history (in which expert after expert warned that we must cut back spending, and fight inflation), after the longest and most intense drafting sessions the committee had endured, and after a prolonged fight on the Senate floor. To see our historic first step to really fight inflation through fiscal policy—through the drafting of a lean budget—thrown down the drain *because of political factors* was one of the most discouraging events of my legislative career.

That the monster has the capacity to grow still more is obvious. But to give you an idea of where that growth will take us, let's assume that federal spending in the 1980s will continue at the rate of the 1970s (that is, that federal spending will *not* match the double digit inflation rate of 1979). If that occurs, in the year 1987, America's federal government will have a $1 trillion budget. If a billion is a number beyond real comprehension, then $1 trillion ($1,000,000,000,000) exists in a galaxy all its own. A top priority is to remedy this excessive growth in federal spending. Congress established, through the historic Budget Reform Act of 1974, a new process designed to bring some discipline to the federal spending system, an initiative which I supported. This new system, establishing budget committees in the House and Senate, unfortunately has had only limited success. Congress as a whole has continually overturned the committees' recommendations.

For example, the failure of Congress to adopt the stringent 1980 budget recommendations of the Senate Budget Committee points up a trend in spending that could spell economic disaster in the '80s. Estimates performed by the Senate Budget Committee late in 1979 showed that, if federal spending trends continued at the rate of the 1970s, the nation would accumulate more than $500 million in deficits during the 1980-1989 period. This ominous development could be avoided only if Congress adopted the principle of reducing federal spending increases to a level below the rate of inflation. That unprecedented recommendation was made by the Senate Budget Committee in the spring of 1979, and was rejected by the full Congress. The Taxpayer's Revolt notwithstanding, Congress hadn't gotten the message.

As the federal government has grown, the private sector has been increasingly strained. Business has suffered an inflation rate higher than any experienced before in peacetime America. Energy costs have soared—in large part due to 20 years of bad government policy. Business has been staggered by literally thousands of government regulations, and yet, business has continued to produce. Profitability in America, however has dropped. The market value of stocks declined more than 60 percent in constant dollars for the entire 1970s. Productivity growth rates slowed, putting America *at the very bottom* among industrialized nations in this category of economic strength, and even sporadically dropped into the negative growth area. Business has shown a resiliency and flexibility of extraordinary proportions, but how much longer can the private sector, facing such odds, continue to give Americans the prosperity they have taken for granted? When will business collapse under these new pressures, which make it impossible for America to achieve either her social goals or to maintain a free and open society.

The first question that comes to my mind as I look into the 1980s is: How did we ever get into such a predicament in the first place?

Significant government intervention in the American economy began as a reaction to the Great Depression. My friend, former Federal Reserve Board Chairman Dr. Arthur Burns, sums up the beginning this way:

> Historically, Americans have had deep faith in the concept of progress—in the idea that it was realistic to expect to better one's own lot and that of one's family in the course of a lifetime. During the greater part of America's history, government intervention in economic life was only peripheral ... the breakdown of economic order during the Great Depression was unprecedented in its scale and scope, and it strained the precept of self-reliance beyond the breaking point. With one-quarter of the labor force unemployed, personal courage and moral stamina could guarantee neither a job nor a livelihood. Succor finally came through a political idea that was novel to a majority of the American people, but compelling nonetheless—namely, that the federal government had a far larger responsibility in the economic sphere than it had hitherto assumed.

Among the chores the federal government now took on with relish were massive public construction projects, work relief, direct relief payments, unemployment insur-

8

ance and old-age pensions, and the beginnings of a massive regulatory effort. Securities, banking, public utilities, housing, and agriculture now felt the heavy hand of an expanded government bureaucracy. In just one decade, the federal government had not only devalued the currency, but had taken upon itself the role of arbiter of such notions as "worthwhile" activities, "harmful" competition, and "unequal" balance of market power.

Into the fray, and benefiting inordinately from it, came economist John Maynard Keynes. Keynes, concentrating on the problem of unemployment, advocated using government expenditures as a sort of "balance wheel" for the economy. Instead of Adam Smith's "Invisible Hand" of the free marketplace, the Keynesians substituted the wisdom of whichever policymakers—and political ideology—controlled the federal government. Inflation was not a central concern for Keynes, since it was of extremely minor significance in the economic picture of his times. For example, inflation had occurred in America only during wartime years until the 1930s, and Great Britain had managed with basically no inflation for the 200 years ending in 1931. Inflation started in this country only after government decided to replace the economic judgments and moral priorities of free persons operating in a relatively free marketplace with economic judgments and moral priorities of its own.

In the complex, resource-scarce times we face ahead, Keynes's ideas must be discarded for a new economic approach. This new approach must recognize that *inflation, not unemployment,* is the curse of the developed nations. Even Keynes himself recognized that, in years of good economic times, inflation-spurring deficits should be avoided. Yet we have ignored this part of his teachings, while listening to other parts of his theories. Perhaps

9

Keynes said it best when he noted, "Practical men, who believe themselves to be quite exempt from any intellectual influences, are usually the slaves of some defunct economist." It has been the indulgence and practicality of politicians, slaves of a defunct economic theory, that has led America to the brink of losing personal and economic freedom.

A sound currency, the free marketplace, and a balanced economy were not the only victims of the Great Depression and reliance on federal antidotes. Above all, personal freedom was diminished. Nobel Prize winning economist F.A. Hayek warned about "the road to serfdom" due to government control, but his words were lost in the hue and cry for new government programs and more government intervention. Economic freedom is an essential part of personal freedom. To the extent that federal policies reduce our economic freedom, those same policies reduce our liberty. For example, if a businessman were to employ ten workers and tell them that, for the first five months of the working year, they would receive no pay, most of us would call that a form of slavery. Yet, when government taxing and spending policies impose essentially that same punishment on every working man and woman in the country, many "expert economists"— who have a vested interest in the *present* system—tell us that it is necessary for a stable economy. Personal rights are abrogated to the interests of the state.

During World War II, the federal government demonstrated that, under certain circumstances, it could guarantee almost full employment. Roosevelt's "Economic Bill of Rights" put the right to a good job at the head of his economic priorities. In 1946, the Congress endorsed the notion that the government ought to provide jobs through the Employment Act. No such emphasis was put on curbing inflation. The right of Americans to have a stable currency was, unfortunately and unnecessarily, sacrificed to the right of Americans to have jobs. This inflationary bias in policy, nurtured by more than 40 years of government action, constitutes the *root economic problem* in our land.

The conclusion of World War II left America as the single most dominant economic and military force in the world. Using our vast economic strength, we rebuilt ravaged Allied nations—and conquered lands as well. At home, rising incomes and large gains in productivity led to increasing consumption and greater leisure. Until the mid-1960s, the prosperity of American families showed improvements. That not all Americans shared to the same extent in this rising prosperity prompted a variety of political crusades: the New Frontier, the War on Poverty, and other such government-inspired efforts to cure all ills afflicting the citizens. It became axiomatic that any perceived problem should be attacked immediately by a government-controlled, taxpayer-financed "program." As identification of social "problems" became a national political pastime, pressure continued, unabated, for more and more government "solutions."

Just as the Great Depression and World War II's onset worked a fundamental change in the relationship between the federal government and the private sector, so did America's efforts to wage both the War on poverty and the war in Vietnam combine to fuel a virulent inflation and set off an extraordinary increase in government economic activity. The choice was not made between "guns" and "butter." The decision was made to continue to try to meet the nation's "tide of rising expectations" *and* to fight the conflict in Southeast Asia—without a tax increase.

11

As the statistics show, the result of government policy has been inflation of an unprecedented level, an almost geometrical increase in expenditures at all levels of government, rising taxation levels, and retrenchment in the average man and woman's quality of life.

Inflation is fast approaching a level in our nation that may force basic changes in our social fabric. In a major address in 1976 Dr. Arthur Burns warned, "In recent years, governments have toppled in Argentina, Chile, and other countries—in large part because the citizens of those countries had lost confidence in the ability of their leaders to cope with the problem of inflation." He noted that many factors are involved in the present inflationary instability, but the *fundamental source* of inflation in our country and in others, he said, is "the lack of discipline in government finances."

Let's examine that last statement closely. It has often been said by critics of federal spending that the fiscal side of government seems "out of control." Twenty years ago that was, by and large, a false statement. The vast majority of spending at federal level was very much within the control of the president and members of Congress. Now, astonishingly, the federal budget is *uncontrollable*, in practical terms! For example, a full 74 percent of federal spending is now classified as uncontrollable by the Congressional Budget Office. Senators and Congressmen have insulated themselves from making tough budget decisions by one of three legislative means: 1) creating programs (called "entitlement programs") that have benefits to which recipients are entitled, regardless of how many persons choose to participate in the program, 2) providing "indexing" for many of these entitlement programs so that increases in benefits go up as inflation increases, and 3) "overselling" the benefits of federal assistance programs so that reform, changes or even attacks on waste within such programs become politically difficult, if not impossible.

This three-part approach to insulating politicians from unpleasant budgetary decisions, developed by politicians themselves, presents the single biggest stumbling-block to budgetary discipline at the federal level.

I remember my own fascination with the entire idea of "uncontrollables." After all, I had been elected in large measure because I was committed to controlling the federal budget. I find it unacceptable to tell my neighbors in New Mexico, "Well, some things are just beyond our control and the federal budget is one of those things." Perhaps the starkest example of the effect of uncontrollables was during the summer of 1979. In the spring of 1979 the deficit projected for the federal government was about $23 billion. Later in 1979 we reviewed probable spending in 1980, and the deficit had soared to almost $30 billion. I asked, "What happened?" A Budget Committee staffer, one of the best in his field, answered mildly, "Inflation has pushed the uncontrollables in the budget so much, Senator, that we have had to add about $6 billion to our projections." The frustration of the budget process was symbolized, for me and many of my Budget Committee colleagues—such as Senator Orrin Hatch of Utah, Senator Rudy Boschwitz of Minnesota, and Senator Bill Armstrong of Colorado—by that one exchange.

Under law, potential beneficiaries of an entitlement program *must be given the benefits*. If the government underestimates the number of beneficiaries of an entitlement program and fails to appropriate sufficient funds, then the Congress must pass what is called a supplemental appropriations midway in the fiscal year, to make sure enough money exists for program recipients. This adds to the deficit and to inflation. It is beyond control, in the sense that until Congress changes the nature and status of the particular program no real fiscal control can be exerted. Very few programs, once enacted, have ever been killed by Congress, no matter how bad they have turned out in the real world.

One entitlement program that is beyond control is the Aid to Families with Dependent Children (AFDC) program. It has grown enormously in its lifetime. It is a classic study of good intentions ending in waste, fraud, abuse, and failure of Congressional oversight. AFDC started back in 1936 (when so many ill-fated programs began), and has grown more than 20-fold in size. More critically, in a 40-year period of almost unbroken economic prosperity this welfare program has encompassed a larger and larger proportion of the nation's children. It originally aided about 1 person in 50 under the age of 18. It now covers almost 1 in every 7 such persons. Nationally, this proportion *more than tripled* between 1960 and 1973. In some of the nation's largest cities, AFDC now covers 1 child out of every 3 under 18 years old.

Yet it is a program that has been widely studied, and a program in which specific legislative, administrative, and operational reforms have been suggested—and few instituted.

My friend Senator Bill Armstrong, Republican from Colorado 2nd, a precise and astute critic of government spending programs, has identified 34 suggested changes in the AFDC program that would yield approximately $3.5 billion in savings, half of that at the federal level, *with no substantial hardship* for eligible recipients. Failure to achieve these savings, Senator Armstrong correctly

14

points out, is a contributing cause to the growing belief Americans hold that welfare fraud and abuse is widespread. As AFDC and other welfare entitlement programs inexorably grow, so does federal domination of the economy, and so does citizen resentment.

Aiding Americans in need is a national tradition of long standing, and a tradition that a moral and just society must continue. But, as the California welfare reform experiment of the early '70s under Governor Reagan showed, these humane ends *can* be reached, even under substantial welfare reform measures. As Congressman Clair Burgner pointed out in 1976, California reduced fraud and abuse, cut back on unnecessary spending, and still helped those who needed help. That is what we must have in the '80s—a moral, just, generous, and efficiently administered governmental system that recognizes a balance between the taxpayer and the recipient of tax dollars.

While the AFDC and other entitlement welfare programs are difficult to change or cut back because Congress has insulated them from real control, even more frustrating to fiscally prudent policymakers is Congress' failure to reform programs that are *not* entitlements. One of the most egregious failures in this area of controllable programs is the now infamous CETA (Comprehensive Education and Training Act) system.

CETA's alleged goal was to use the power of the federal government to get jobs to the unemployed in times of economic downturns. Congress adopted this program despite the misgivings of many of us that such "makework" federal jobs would ever accomplish the goal, especially since we had the vast numbers of private-sector jobs that have been created by an expanding economy for much less money. Despite the most broad-based eco-

15

nomic expansion in American history, CETA grew and grew, consuming more than $10 billion a year at its height. CETA survived attacks in studies by the General Accounting Office and the Brookings Institution. Despite criticism from every level, CETA prospered.

In early 1978, even the Labor Department was forced to reveal that more than 11 percent of the public service participants under CETA were either ineligible or of undetermined eligibility. Later, it was shown that only 8 percent of the Title VI CETA funds available for the projected fiscal year 1980 budget were going to distressed cities, the very places in which most unemployment occurred. But CETA's protectors are well-placed, and it has survived all these assaults, spending billions a year for jobs that lead nowhere, teach little, and serve mainly to give street politicians another pulpit from which to preach.

CETA is a prototypical program. The belief that federal intervention can end all unemployment, train all persons, and provide a meaningful and future-oriented job for everyone (even those choosing not to work at all), led to creation of the CETA program. The constituency of beneficiaries from CETA programs—mayors, special interest group leaders, county and city commissioners, professional liberals—make cutbacks in the program extremely difficult politically.

CETA fulfills many of the mandates of the "uncontrollable" program. CETA was founded on unrealistic promises by politicians, sold to a public with high expectations, given a broad base of support by the congressional mandate that all prime sponsors in all areas would receive monies, and increased in size as inflation went up (although the program was supposed to be related to unemployment, which declined). Fortunately, CETA is not an entitlement program and *can* be controlled if

16

Congress demonstrates the will. Only through the heroic efforts of Republican senators such as Senator Henry Bellmon of Oklahoma and hard-nosed fiscal conservatives such as Florida's Senator Lawton Chiles, a Democrat, were Senate attacks against CETA launched in the late 1970s.

The key to reforming AFDC or CETA, indeed the key to changing fiscal policy at the federal level, is congressional action. Laws must be changed. A fundamental shift must occur in the way *Congress* does business. Reorganizing the bureaucracy won't help: federal agencies merely enforce and interpret the legislation Congress gives them.

The only real solution is for Congress to stop overstating the government's ability to satisfy a tide of rising expectations, and to tell Americans what most Americans already know: limits exist to what the federal government can do. Congress must recognize that government should do less, and do that "less" better. Congress must begin the long task of fundamentally changing tax laws, reviewing and changing entitlement and other aid programs, and cutting federal outlays. I think this mammoth task is a realistic one. I think we can take concrete steps to begin the job.

We have experienced during the past fifteen years: a rate of inflation in double digit range (greater than 13 percent in 1979); persistent unemployment of more than 5½ percent (and often soaring to more than 8 percent); a tax burden, for federal programs alone, of almost 22 percent of the Gross National Product; seriously declining productivity; an interest rate of only a little more than 5 percent on personal savings (the capital so necessary to our economy); a drop in real wages for the average worker; and a rise in government spending, with its in-

17

flationary bias, producing a huge cumulative deficit during the past decade. Such is the legacy of our government's "demand side" economic policies, coupled with the growing recognition of resource scarcity.

Compounding the problem is a regulatory zeal that creates enormous additional costs to business. As an example, I cite the following figures of Murray L. Weidenbaum, Director of the Center for the Study of American Business at Washington University, St. Louis. His work indicates that federal, state, and local government regulations hike the cost of a new home by between $1,500 and and $2,500. In the aggregate, Weidenbaum writes, "the cost to business of complying with federal regulation came to $75.4 billion in 1977. Those costs are inevitably passed on to the consumer in the form of higher prices." He also calculated that the cost of federally-mandated safety and environmental features increased the cost of the average passenger car by $666 in 1978.

Dr. Weidenbaum talks in scholarly terms, but let me put things in personal terms for a moment. In the first decade of this century, an Italian man left his home country to seek opportunity in America. Like so many others, he had found it almost impossible to truly improve his like in the chaos of his native land. America held out the beacon of hope and opportunity. This young man married another Italian immigrant, and they started a small corner grocery in Albuquerque, then a small community in the territory of New Mexico. That man was my father, as you may have guessed, and I remember the hours I spent with him, stocking the shelves and watching him work seven days a week to realize his dream. At night he would share with us over the dinner table the joys of the day—a new truck, another new employe, the great move to a new location, the first warehouse.

I regret to say this, but the things my fathered offered to his customers to get and keep their trust—good service, competitive prices, honest goods—would not be enough, in this day and age. After all, he was small, and was potential prey for the very large grocery chains. Indeed, because only the very large can succeed in the regulation-bound climate of the present economic scene, the small entrepreneur has been forced out. I know that my father could never have afforded a bookkeeper or a lawyer to make sure he had complied with esoteric federal regulations or to make costly—but most cosmetic—changes in the workplace to satisfy a bureaucrat in Washington. No, I suspect that my father, for all his hard work and honesty, *would have failed* in this new climate. And that simple fact, I suspect, summarizes a lot of what's wrong with our economic system today.

We have now a federal government that has subsidized consumption of food, housing, health care, education, and other goods and services through a growing and unresponsive hodgepodge of entitlement programs, grants and tax policies biased against savings and investment. It has imposed a further burden on the productive side of the economy through massive regulation. What is an agenda for the future that will bring a new prosperity to America?

The key word in that last sentence is "prosperity." Congressman Jack Kemp, Republican from Buffalo, New York, notes that we can all devise a plan that will bring a new *austerity* to the nation, and I concur; indeed, I argue that the economic program of the Carter Administration and the Democratic majority in Congress *guarantees* a new austerity for the average working man and woman,

19

for the small businessman—and eventually, economic catastrophe for the poor, the elderly, and the unemployed. Inflation is the beginning of the catastrophe, but looming ahead could be a collapse of the inflationary economy into a prolonged and disastrous depression that will deny to almost everyone the quality of life we have a right to expect from the richest nation on earth. *Avoiding* such a catastrophe, and the inevitable social tensions it will bring with it, stands as the chief challenge to policymakers in the next decade.

Here is my agenda for a new prosperity. Many of these notions have been urged before by my Republican colleagues in the Congress, so I claim no unique authorship. However, my work on the Senate Budget Committee for the past five years persuades me that these ideas deserve serious consideration. Some of them are absolutely essential.

CUTTING AND REFORMING TAXES

In my judgment, the single most important step that must be taken is a substantial, fundamental reform of the nation's tax laws. Simply talking about a cut in personal income tax rates is not enough, though such a reduction *is* an important part of the overhaul of the tax laws that I recommend. Former Republican-Conservative Senator James Buckley of New York and Republican Secretary of the Treasury, Bill Simon, have called for a 10 percent income tax rate and elimination of all exemptions. Senator Bill Roth of Delaware and Congressman Jack Kemp have continually advocated across-the-board tax cuts in a variety of proposals. The Republican party membership within the Senate has specifically endorsed substantial cuts and reform of the tax system. Out of

20

these various ideas, certain basic principles seem critical to a tax system that encourages *prosperity*, not austerity:

1. A real cut in personal and business income tax rates at a level at least sufficient within each tax bracket to offset "bracket creep," the phenomenon that sends us all into higher tax brackets because of inflation. The size of this cut may be in the range of the 10 percent a year cut advocated by Kemp-Roth II (introduced in January of 1979 and supported by many of us with the Republican party).

2. A real tax cut greater than the amount contained in the Kemp-Roth proposal over the next several years, including a substantial cut in business taxes for new businesses and small businesses, and a smaller cut in *all* business taxes.

3. Continuing rapid depreciation tax policies for business and innovative use of the tax code to encourage business to hire and train new employes.

4. Innovative tax provisions to spur capital formation; to increase productivity, research, and development; and to encourage personal savings.

Some argue that tax cuts without spending cuts might increase inflationary pressures within the federal budget by increasing the federal deficit. The debate over "supply side" economics—which put a premium on cutting taxes, so that production within the economy is encouraged—has been going on in a significant manner since 1976. On one side stand such economists as Michael Evans of Chase Econometrics, who argue that the increased prosperity from a straight tax cut would yield more revenues to the government, and a smaller deficit. They point to the Kennedy tax cut of the early 1960s and the prosperity it brought as an example of what the enactment of Kemp-

Roth II would do. Other Conservative economists, such as Murray L. Weidenbaum, have judged that "it is doubtful whether those revenue increases would fully offset the effect of the lower rates." However, a tax cut of real size, and indexing of the tax code for the future, would have one fundamental consequence: government would have fewer of our tax dollars to play with and *would have to begin to institute reforms,* make basic decisions on priorities, and decrease the rate of increase in government spending and government intervention in our economy. A tax cut could be the first step in a return to a freer marketplace in which individual free citizens making economic decisions, each day in their lives determine the nation's economy.

LIMITING GOVERNMENT SPENDING

My second priority is limiting the amount of federal spending, even if we must someday resort to the extreme notion of a Constitutional Amendment to balance the federal budget except in times of emergency situations.

Back in 1969, Federal Reserve Board Chairman Dr. Arthur Burns noted with alarm that the federal budget would soon pass the $200 billion mark, fueled by extraordinary increases in social program spending. He called this trend "explosive," and warned that it had led to predictable and widespread inefficiencies within government agencies that had been created, handed billions of dollars in a short period of time, and mandated to meet certain social goals. Professor Burns concluded, "In view of the explosive growth of federal spending and the ineffectiveness or inefficiency of much of it, I am inclined to think that the need for expenditure reform may be even greater than the need for tax reform." If you merely changed many of the numbers that Dr. Burns cited in that speech to the Tax Foundation, you would find that his prophecies are as true today as they were then. Unfortunately, Congress has not listened nor adopted the spending reforms that he and many since him have recommended.

Here are some of the positive proposals that other Republicans and I have recommended, and which have been endorsed by a wide range of economists:

1. Impose a statutory, binding limitation on the percentage of our Gross National Product that the federal government can spend. At present, federal spending is approximately 22 percent of GNP (it was less than 18.5 percent in 1960). The trend has been for spending to constitute an even larger percentage of GNP, despite the fact that the nation enjoyed greater real prosperity in those years when the spending proportion was smaller. I believe the maximum allowable percentage should be 19 percent. For those who believe that 1 percent is a small matter, remember that 1 percent of the GNP in 1979 would have been approximately \$25 billion. We could have removed the entire deficit for that year, if we had required that government spending comprise no more than 19 percent of the GNP..

2. Mandate through statute that a balanced budget for the federal government be achieved in those years of real GNP growth, except in emergency circumstances.

3. Require that agencies of the federal government that are presently "off-budget" be put on the federal budget to accurately reflect the total role and intervention of the federal government in our economy, and

to prevent circumvention of the budget through the use of loan guarantees and other credit mechanisms.

4. Require—through use of the so-called Sunset concept or other mandated form of congressional review —reforms and even repeal of government spending programs, including entitlements. Such a provision would put great pressure on the Congress to achieve savings through reforms that, some experts believe, could reduce federal spending by as much as 10 percent of the total government budget each year. The list of possible reforms, savings, and antifraud efforts— in such programs as Social Security, public assistance, Medicaid, Medicare, federal pension programs and other transfer payment systems—is enormous.

5. Deregulate many presently-regulated industries to allow the free marketplace, with its inherent efficiencies, to operate, and to reduce expenditures for the burgeoning bureaucracy within agencies.

6. Increase the use of consolidated bloc grant approaches, rather than the tangle of hundreds of categorical grants that now blot tens of thousands of pages of the federal law. Consolidation of grants would encourage efficiency, reduce federal bureaucracy, give flexibility to local and state government to make priority decisions based upon indigenous circumstances and, importantly, make cuts in such programs more easily possible within the federal budgetary process.

7. Begin a process that I call "refederalization." This process would bring out the fact that certain things *can be done better* at the local level by local and state governments than by the federal government from Washington, D.C. Those problems that are truly local in nature (welfare of citizens, education, and law en-

forcement) would be done at the local level, while truly national chores (national defense, foreign policy) would remain national tasks. My preliminary analysis shows that several billions of dollars would be "transferred" in this manner. Eventually, if the state and local governments decided that a particular task were not needed in their area at the time, they could stop the program, saving tax dollars. This kind of flexibility, mentioned in proposal 6 above, would truly revitalize the federal system and stop the inexorable drive towards more and more centralization.

8. Amend the Congressional Budget Reform Act to incorporate multi-year budgeting, a longer period between authorizations and appropriations legislation, and require a binding spending ceiling in the First Concurrent Budget Resolution. Congress can—and has—ignored the Budget Committee. But putting more teeth in these committees is a small step toward fiscal responsibility and discipline, and a necessary one if pressure on Congress for fiscal restraint is to be maintained.

RESTORE AMERICA TO INDIVIDUAL AMERICANS

Fundamental to a real resurgence in this nation's well-being is recognition that we have prospered in the past because we have a free enterprise system based upon innovation, initiative, regard for personal achievement, and freedom for persons within our society to pursue their dreams as they see fit. A free economic system is crucial to restoring the American Dream. Since the 1930s, we have lost sight of *how* America became great, how so many Americans have prospered. We have substituted the faulty and self-serving "wisdom" of officeholders in Washington, D.C., for the wisdom of free people in a free market. As we confront the severe resource shortages and international challenges of the 1980s, we must return to the private sector and to the incredible energy of the free enterprise system.

For example, this nation has an energy shortage. Many plans involving government spending and control have been offered to solve this problem (despite the fact that government intervention in our energy economy has been one of the prime causes of the present problem). Greater reliance on the free market system, with occasional partnerships between the federal government and private firms, stands as the only sensible long-range solution. Yet already we hear, once again, the call for controls and regulation, for disincentives to domestic production of energy. Such strategies have failed in the past, and are destined to fail in the future.

Many of my Republican Senate colleagues will concern themselves with the proper approach to solving our energy problems, as well as other challenges of the '80s presented in this book. But at the bottom of all their recommendations will be the belief that individual Amercans, motivated by a desire to improve their lot, *can* solve those challenges *if given the freedom* to do so. To a Democratic Congress too long imbued with the notion that the people are to be distrusted, and that in government programs lies our only salvation, such emphasis on individual initiative and the free market system will be bitter medicine. *Without* a large dose of that medicine, however, we will not bequeath to our children the improved quality of life they have every right to expect.

DEFENSE
U.S. NATIONAL SECURITY POLICY

By SENATOR JAKE GARN

Throughout my adult life, I have been concerned that we maintain the security of our country, and the liberties that are every American's right. When I was a pilot in the U.S. Navy, I viewed firsthand our nation's determination to protect itself and the entire free world. Later, as mayor of Salt Lake City, I quite frankly took it for granted that the proper safeguards were being taken to counter any conceivable threat to the well-being of the United States and its vital interests. I was sadly mistaken.

This painful awareness has been confirmed many times over since I first came to the United States in 1974. Through my membership on the Armed Services Committee, the Appropriations Committee, and the Select Committee on Intelligence, I have witnessed the undeniable evidence of the great military, economic, and political dangers facing our nation. You, the public, have experienced firsthand the dangers of economic strangulation, as you waited in long gas lines or pondered the thought of how to heat your homes.

Unfortunately, in light of President Carter's decision to underfund our general purpose forces, to cancel the B-1 Bomber and the neutron warhead, to delay deployment of the Trident submarine and the MX mobile ICBM and the Cruise missile, to sign a flawed SALT II Treaty, and to respond timidly to Soviet adventurism, many Americans, as well as our friends abroad, are now questioning whether or not the United States is taking the necessary steps to check a growing variety of threats posed by the Soviet Union and her proxies (such as the Cubans and East Germans) against the free world. The Soviet military threat, however, did not just spring to life. Rather it has systematically emerged over the past decade, by means of the greatest arms buildup the world has ever seen. On the other hand, U.S. national security policy has been one of *unilateral restraint*.

As we enter the 1980s, the question we must ask ourselves is whether we will allow the adverse trends affecting our security to continue, or whether we will revive American purpose and determination in the face of a number of critical challenges. I believe that it is essential for *the public* to consider the dilemmas facing our national security. Only then will our nation be able to make the difficult decisions that lie ahead.

This is a book about the promise of Conservatism. However, in addressing what the future could hold in the '80s for America's national security, I can make only one promise: unless the defense policies characteristic of the first three years of the Carter Administration are reversed, and a new direction taken, the United States will decline rapidly into a second-rate power. We will have barely enough strength to keep the wolves from our own front door, let alone defend the rest of the free world. While the Administration in late 1979 came forward, after strong urging by the Senate, with a stronger defense agenda, its commitment seems at best to be lukewarm.

It would be easy and politically useful to stop here

and blame the bleak prospects on the present Administration. To be honest, though, that would not be fair. Things have gotten worse under the present Administration; I can't deny that. But the problem is deeper than the party or personality of the sitting president, and it goes back before his name was even a household word in Georgia.

It started, ironically enough, after World War II, with one of the most noble and humanitarian collective acts in the history of mankind. At that pivotal moment, America had the largest army, the strongest navy, the best air forces, and the best weapons and equipment of any nation on earth. Our economy was intact, gearing itself to break out into consumer production, but still capable of fueling the huge war machine. For the first time in history, one nation—ours—had the military and economic strength to literally take over the world. But what did we "Yankee imperialists" do? We repaired the damage of the war; we restored the economies of Europe and Japan; we literally rebuilt the empires of the enemies we had just destroyed. We demobilized our armies and demilitarized our economy. We became the crutch for the world as it limped back from the brink of destruction.

Now, like the crutch no longer needed when the cripple learns to walk, we are cast aside, out of sight and barely remembered for the help we gave before the injuries healed. I suppose that is not all bad. After all, we didn't do it for the credit. We did it for the betterment of our fellow man. So we shouldn't really care if the world has forgotten about it. But *we* shouldn't forget it. We should be proud—not boastful, but proud—of what we were able to do, and what our motivation was to do it. We should remember that America is capable of greatness; that it has an obligation, thrust upon it by virtue of its leadership in that terrible World War and by its supporting role in the aftermath of that conflict, to have something to say about the course of world history.

Otherwise, there is no point in writing this chapter. There is no point in discussing anything about national security beyond how big a fence we can build around America.

Other chapters of this book describe the great challenges facing our society in domestic, economic, and social terms. They describe the limitations of our nation's resources and the need to define more efficient, effective programs within the framework of sound and sensible priorities. Consequently, the question is often asked: must we spend so much for guns when we are in such desperate need of butter? Unfortunately, to answer that question with a "No" requires a dreamworld that simply doesn't fit reality. I wish that were not the case. We all do. No moral, thinking person can take any pleasure from the design and creation of weapons of destruction. But the lion and the lamb have yet to learn to lie down together in peace. We have enemies in the world; yes they do seek the destruction of America and the ideals of freedom and democracy that our nation represents. I have always thought that was an obvious fact of life. But I am surprised at how widespread the feelings of complacency are today.

Two years ago I spoke to a group of students at a small college in northern Louisiana. I was discussing the military balance between the U.S. and the Soviet Union. When I took questions from the audience, the first one was, "Senator, do you really believe the Soviet Union would ever attack the United States?" The student obviously did not, as indicated by the tone of his voice, and I could tell from the expressions and nods of a number of others in the auditorium that many of them shared his scepticism. They had grown up with "detente," and nothing else seemed reasonable.

The cold, hard facts, however, do not support the hopes of that student, and explode the myth of detente. There is a real threat to the security of the United States in the massive Soviet arms build-up which has occurred during the past ten years. They have amassed tremendous power, and have never denied their intention to use it to promote global communism. Over the past 10 years of detente and peaceful coexistence, they have been more subtle than was Mr. Khrushchev, when he blurted out his intention to "bury" us. But their long-term objectives have not changed.

What are some of the facts on which I base my assertion that there is a Soviet threat to our national security?

No threat can exist unless there is vulnerability. Consequently, to fully understand the threat, we need to talk first about our vulnerabilities. The issue obviously is more complex than this, but for the sake of argument, I will say that there are two major areas in which the United States is increasingly vulnerable: in the military sphere, and the economic sphere.

THE MILITARY VULNERABILITIES

America's military power generally consists of three major components: Strategic (intercontinental), Theater (regional), and General Purpose forces.

"Strategic" forces, for the most part, consist of nuclear weapons and the devices necessary to deliver them to a target, such as a missile, a bomber or a submarine. The primary purpose of nuclear weapons has not changed since the first bombs were dropped on Hiroshima and Nagasaki. Their purpose is to present a believable threat of horrible massive destruction. Japan did not surrender because the two bombs disrupted important strategic industries or destroyed Japan's military machine. She surrendered to avoid any more of the horrors of atomic destruction that the United States very obviously had the capability—and the willingness—to deliver. The bombs acted as a deterrent, then, against any further hostilities by the Japanese. That is essentially their purpose today, although the precise nature of their threat depends largely on the sorts of targets they are aimed at and, of course, on their ability to destroy those targets.

For some time the United States had clear nuclear superiority, and there was no challenge to her ability to deter aggression. The Cuban Crisis of 1962 was a perfect example of how "rattling the nuclear saber" forced the Soviet Union to abandon its attempt to place missiles in Cuba. Now, however, we are faced with a world in which there are *two* nuclear superpowers, and four other nations with the proven potential to build and deliver nuclear weapons. Eight or ten other nations are moving in that direction. The influence of nuclear weapons is not so clear anymore. Threats have to be balanced against each other. This has resulted in the development of the theory of Mutual Assured Destruction—or "MAD"—on which we have based our development of strategic forces.

Put simply, MAD says that "We" will not attack "Them" because "They" will be able to hit us back harder than we can stand. As long as both—or all—of the nuclear powers can make that statement, then it's a standoff, and deterrence has succeeded. The problem with MAD is that the assurance of destruction must continue to be "Mutual." When it is not, the country that is perceived to be weaker is more vulnerable to attack, or—at the very least—to nuclear blackmail, by the

32

stronger country. The important question for the '80s, then, is whether the two superpowers have an equal capability to destroy each other.

Most analysts agree that today, in early 1980, the balance of forces is roughly equal. They call it "parity," or "rough equivalence." I don't really quarrel with that assessment. The Soviets have some advantages over us and we have some offsetting advantages over them. But such comparisons cannot be made once and forgotten. The arsenals change, both in quality and in quantity, and we must examine them continually, taking into account expected technological breakthroughs and development trends. Looking at the 1979 arsenals and expected trends which are consistent with the terms of SALT II, the comparative strategic posture between 1979 and 1985 looks like this:

U.S. vs. SOVIET STRATEGIC FORCE MEASURES

	1979		1985	
	US	USSR	US	USSR
Launchers (ICBMs, SLBMS bombers)	2,053	2,504	2,130	2,246
Warheads	9,514	8,226	12,504	11,728
Megatonnage (millions of tons of TNT)	3,253	7,836	3,537	10,870
Throwweight (millions of lbs.)	7.51	12.15	7.93	14.45

Source: *Statement of the Honorable Paul Nitze,* Hearings before Senate Foreign Relations Committee, PART I, page 439.

As the table shows, the one advantage we have in 1979—the number of warheads—is almost eliminated by 1985. On the other hand, the Soviet advantage in total megatonnage, or destructive power, increases. If the

Backfire Bomber is included in the Soviet measurements —as it should be, we suffer a serious disadvantage in *all* of the key measurements of strategic power represented in the above chart.

The Soviet advantages in numbers is compounded by expected qualitative disparities that will develop, particularly with regard to strategic bombers. The cause? Our failure to replace the aging B-52 bombers with the B-1 bomber. We spent $4.5 billion to develop this plane and then President Carter canceled its production, *without gaining any concessions* from the Soviets in return. Not only is this bad negotiating, it is bad defense planning. The B-1 is a superb penetrating aircraft and should have gone into production. I know a little something about combat airplanes, having been a military pilot for twenty years. A year ago I flew one of the B-1 prototypes. It is an incredible sensation, believe me, to be flying at almost the speed of sound (and yet only about half as fast as the plane can actually fly), a mere 200 feet above the waves of the Pacific Ocean, rushing directly at the oncoming cliffs of the shore, with no need to have a hand on the controls. The terrain-following radar that guides the B-1 knows when to lift the nose up and steer the plane clear of any large, solid object, like a mountain. It is a beautiful, capable airplane, and one of the great mistakes of this Administration was to clip its wings.

Perhaps the most threatening improvement made by the Soviets is in the accuracy of their land-based ICBMs (intercontinental ballistic missiles). The ability to more accurately target, or aim, large powerful warheads greatly increases their threat against the sort of heavy, reinforced underground silos from which missiles are launched. The Soviet Union is rapidly approaching the type of accuracy necessary to destroy our missile silos. On top of that, they have much larger missiles, which can carry a larger number of massive warheads than our missiles. The preceding chart illustrates the numerical advantage the Soviets will have in warheads and megatonnage by 1985; this makes their improved accuracy that much more of a threat to our land-based ICBM force.

It is absolutely necessary that an answer be found to the threatened vulnerability of our land-based Minuteman ICBMs. The solution that has been proposed is to develop a new land-based missile that can be moved around. By not giving the Soviets a stationary target, a mobile missile will reduce the vulnerability of our missile force and discourage the Soviets from considering a first strike against our land-based ICBM system. The new missile has come to be known as the "MX," or "Missile Experimental." It has been under development for several years, and is a long overdue addition to our strategic forces. Apart from the missile itself—which is larger than the Minuteman and capable of carrying up to ten warheads, instead of one or three our Minuteman carry—there is the question of how it is to be stored, moved around, and launched.

In other words, what will the "basing mode" be for the MX? This question has not yet been answered. President Carter has proposed a basing mode that consists of a large paved oval, or "racetrack," with twenty-three horizontal shelters located at different points around the track. Each one could contain and launch a missile. The MX missile assigned to each "racetrack" would be moved around from shelter to shelter on a random basis, the idea being that the Soviets wouldn't know from one moment to the next precisely which shelter housed a missile, and would therefore be unable to reliably target a warhead against the MX.

The "shell game" idea, as it has been called, is basically a good idea. I am not convinced, however, that the "racetrack" basing mode is the best choice. There are serious questions about the funding and development of that sort of basing mode, especially within the states where the system might be built, such as my own state of Utah. Those questions have to be resolved, as well as the fundamental issue of which basing mode makes the most military sense. Once these preliminary concerns are resolved and the development and construction of the system gets started, it will still take several years before a bottle of champagne can be broken over it.

It is important, therefore, that these decisions be made as quickly as possible, and that the Congress and this Administration—or any subsequent one—keep up the effort to complete the system. We simply *don't have the luxury* of long delays. It would make the system too expensive, and it would prolong the period that our ICBM forces would remain vulnerable. We cannot afford either.

The same should be said about the new weapons systems that are joining our strategic forces: the Trident submarine, and the Trident II SLBM (sea-launched ballistic missile). The strength of our sea-based deterrent would be undercut if they are delayed any longer in production. The Trident submarine—which is scheduled to replace our aging Polaris and Poseiden submarines by 1985—is already 2-3 years behind schedule. Further delay must be avoided.

There are two other aspects of strategic power that ought to be mentioned before moving on to the Theater nuclear forces: Civil Defense and so-called exotic weapons research. In both, we lag considerably behind the Soviet Union.

The U.S. spends about $100 million a year for civil

defense; the Soviets spend ten times that amount. They are serious about civil defense and much of their money goes for construction of shelters that can resist atomic blasts. It is estimated that by 1988 they will be able to shelter something like thirty million people in urban areas in these facilities. We have nothing comparable in the U.S., and no plans to build any. (In fact, we are told that an aggressive civil defense program would be a "dangerously provocative act" that the Soviets wouldn't like, so we mustn't do it.)

My own attitude towards civil defense is that right now it is a necessity that *has to take a back seat* to a greater necessity. We have limited funds, and I would prefer to use them to first develop the hard military strength we need in both the strategic and conventional defense areas. The best civil defense system in the world is still no substitute for a credible deterrent, and that comes from having the kinds of strategic hardware I have been talking about. If we "keep a lot of powder, and keep it dry," we stand a better chance of never needing blast shelters.

"Exotic weapons" are the stuff of "Star Wars"; they are weapons of the future—and yet the not too distant future. The United States has held back in conducting research into these kinds of weapons, hoping to avoid an arms race in this very expensive and highly technical area. But the Soviets, true to form, have not demonstrated any similar restraint. They are outspending us five-to-one in this area.

Due to our limited intelligence capabilities in the USSR, we have little chance of knowing if the Soviets are close to a technical breakthrough. Superiority in this sort of weapon could have a great effect on the overall balance of power. Laser and directed-energy weapons could be invaluable as an antisatellite or even as an anti-ballistic-missile (ABM) system. A knowledge and understanding of this complex but important field is something we cannot allow the Soviets to monopolize.

In talking about "Theater" forces, we are generally referring to the forces that are available for the defense of Europe and the NATO alliance. Our commitment to maintain the integrity of the Atlantic Alliance (NATO) is an important cornerstone of our national security policy. Through that alliance, we have linked the destiny of America with the destiny of Europe, and vice versa. It is the single most important alliance this nation has, and its continued strength after thirty years is a tribute to all NATO members.

In late August, 1979, I attended a conference in Brussels, Belgium, on the subject of "NATO: The Next Thirty Years." Although there was a general feeling of optimism about the future stability of NATO, serious questions were raised about the specific role of the United States in providing nuclear deterrence. During the years of U.S. nuclear superiority, the "umbrella" of our power extended to our allies in NATO. They knew that we would consider an attack on any of them the same as an attack on us, and we would respond accordingly. Many of the Europeans at the conference wanted to know if the "umbrella" still covered them. Many were concerned about the vulnerability of the "umbrella" for the same reasons I have already mentioned. There was a consensus that the tired, old doctrine of MAD was, in fact, tired and old and mad, or insane. Even those who didn't want to admit that MAD was a mistaken concept at least had to agree that it does not apply to the real world of today.

I was glad to see so many prominent figures from the NATO countries beginning to recognize the changing strategic environment. It gave me great hope for the ability of NATO to respond in a united way to the challenges of the '80s. It is important to remember one other point that I heard over and over again in Brussels: whatever is done to strengthen NATO, the United States *must take the lead*. Our European partners are prepared to do their part, but only if we are prepared to lead the way.

It is pretty well recognized now that the theater nuclear balance has shifted against NATO and in favor of the Warsaw Pact countries. The Alliance's virtual monopoly on tactical nuclear weapons has disappeared. This has happened at a time when theater nuclear strength is especially important to help offset the vulnerability of U.S. strategic, land-based ICBMs. The NATO Alliance has recognized this fact and has approved a program to improve and modernize theater nuclear forces. *Improvements* are necessary to offset the superior, and continuously improving, Soviet theater nuclear capabilities.

The Warsaw Pact has a depth and dispersion of capacity in this field. They have nuclear launchers at the division level, which can be moved rapidly around a battle front in support of the division to which they are assigned. In addition, the Pact has longer-range nuclear systems that can attack points in Europe from the western border areas of the Soviet Union. These systems are being modernized by replacement with new mobile SS-20 medium-range ballistic missiles. They also have submarines and surface ships armed with ballistic missiles and cruise missiles. On top of that, the Soviet Backfire bomber, which can even attack the U.S. from bases in Russia, is available for use in the European theater. It is a very powerful and capable bomber and can play a decisive role as a means of delivering nuclear weapons. The U.S. and NATO don't have anything like these capabilities at the present time. It is a vacuum that must be filled.

In addition to superior weapons and nuclear delivery vehicles, the Warsaw Pact has an advantage in training, and in the preparation and equipping of its forces to fight in a nuclear and/or chemical war. Contrary to prevailing western practice, the Soviets do *not* consider nuclear war to be unthinkable. Their military doctrine, in fact, stresses the probability of escalation to nuclear war from any of a variety of armed hostilities that might occur in Europe and elsewhere. The Soviet Union intends to be prepared to fight, win, *and survive* a nuclear war. Their entire military posture is designed on that basis and the Warsaw Pact forces are no different. They can drive their tanks and personnel carriers into a contaminated area and function effectively with sophisticated protective devices built into their equipment. Since we can't imagine anyone ever really using nuclear or chemical weapons, we haven't prepared very well for their effects on a battlefield.

We face many challenges in the next decade, but none is more important than restoring the theater nuclear balance in NATO. We can't afford to neglect our commitment to the Alliance, because it is already such a tempting target for the Soviet Union. The Soviets would like nothing more than to see NATO's nuclear vulnerability continue to grow to the point where the Warsaw Pact superiority in theater nuclear forces is equal to their traditional and expanding superiority in conventional forces.

As the name suggests, "General Purpose" forces are designed for a variety of tasks in a variety of situations.

When we refer to "conventional" forces, it is general purpose forces that we are talking about. They are non-nuclear and basically made up of the men and women in blue, green or khaki and their arms and equipment. They are active-duty forces, reserve units and National Guard units. They are older than the U.S. itself, and continue to be our first and best line of defense.

The U.S. General Purpose Forces are made up of four major categories of forces: *land, tactical air, naval,* and *mobility* forces. The Soviets have a general purpose forces war machine that is made up of similar elements. It is bigger than that of the United States, and on the way to becoming better. The Soviets outspend the U.S. in this area by about two-to-one.

Since 1964, Soviet ground forces have grown from about 1.4 million men to over 2 million. (About 460,000 border guards and militarized internal security forces are not counted in these totals.) Total Soviet divisions have increased from about 150 to over 170, and many Soviet forward deployed divisions have increased their manpower and equipment levels by 10-20%. Soviet tactical air forces have added 1400 aircraft and 24 regiments.

Soviet naval forces have decreased slightly in number, as many small patrol vessels have been retired, but the proportion of larger and more capable ships has risen dramatically. The Soviet Navy has deployed two KIEV-class light VTOL (vertical takeoff and landing) carriers (and they are building two more, plus their first large, full-size aircraft carrier), two MOSKVA class ASW (antisubmarine warfare) carriers, about 270 surface combatants—about 20 armed with cruise missiles, almost 200 attack submarines and over 60 cruise missile submarines, about 100 amphibious warfare ships, and approximately 300 support ships. Long range airlift, or mobility forces, also have not grown in numbers, but they are improved in quality and range. The offensive and defensive chemical warfare capabilities of Soviet forces have improved and they are dramatically better than similar U.S. and NATO capabilities.

The *land forces of the U.S.* are not very large; we have 16 active army divisions, 8 National Guard divisions, 21 active and reserve brigades, and three active and one reserve Marine Corps divisions. They are stationed worldwide, but we still rely heavily on our allies to provide the bulk of land forces that are required for our collective defense.

As we enter the 1980s the number of U.S. divisions is simply *not adequate*. We do not have enough forces to meet the requirements of a major conflict with the Soviet Union such as in the NATO Theater, preceded by a minor conflict elsewhere—the Middle East, for example.

The *tactical air forces* of the U.S. consist of active, Reserve, and National Guard Air Force units, active and Reserve Navy units, and active and Reserve Marine Corps units. The U.S. Air Force has 26 active and 11 Reserve/Guard wings, and 42 active/Reserve/Guard special mission squadrons. Naval tactical Air Forces are based with our 12 carriers—one active tactical air wing per carrier and two reserve wings. The Marine Corps has 3 active and one Reserve tactical air wing.

These forces are designed to fight day or night and in adverse weather conditions. Their missions are to maintain air superiority, provide air defense, make strikes deep into enemy territory, provide close air support for ground combat operations, assist in intelligence collection, conduct electronic warfare, provide in-flight refueling for sustained action, and conduct early warning and control missions. A large variety of aircraft perform these missions, and each Service has developed tactics and aircraft to meet the needs of each specialized mission. Our pilots and equipment are good, although they are very expensive. I have flown many of the aircraft that make up our tactical air forces, and I know we have a force to be proud of. We are doing the right kinds of things in this area, we *just need to do more.*

I might add that my experience has also shown me that the best equipment is still subject to the human frailties of its operator. My first flight in an F-14 from the deck of an aircraft carrier two years ago had to be cut short when I developed a "charlie horse" in my leg. My chair on the floor of the Senate bears no resemblance, of course, to the tight cockpit seat of an F-14, so it didn't provide me with the right kind of exercise to prepare me for the flight. Certainly, proper training and conditioning can eliminate that kind of problem, and we must provide the necessary funding for training our pilots.

The U.S. Navy—active and reserve—is comprised of 479 ships: 12 active aircraft carriers, 194 surface combatants, 77 nuclear attack submarines, 68 amphibious warfare ships, 25 mine warfare ships, and 102 support ships. It is the glue that binds our alliance structures together, and our alliances provide us with an opportunity to defend our nation far from our own shores with help of other nations which share our values of freedom and democracy.

The Navy, for all of its importance in our national strategy, is in serious trouble. Its capability to carry out assigned missions is marginal. The number of ships has declined from over 900 in 1968 to 479 today. Of those, many have serious maintenance problems, most are aging, and many do not have modernized weapons systems, radars, or command and control equipment.

43

In a day and age when so many of our vital commodities, especially oil supplies, must be imported from across the oceans, the ability to control the seas is vital. Others in this book have discussed the problems of dependency on foreign sources for vital goods, and much can and, I hope, will be done to reduce the level of our dependency. In the meantime, however, open sea lanes are the umbilical cords that help sustain our life as a nation. To have them cut by superior enemy naval power may not be fatal, but would most certainly be critical at least through the decade of the '80s.

Our *mobility forces,* obviously, are the forces necessary to move land forces around and to keep them supplied with equipment, material, and reinforcements. These forces consist of: strategic airlift forces (70 C-5A and 234 C-41 aircraft); sealift forces (27 Military Sealift Command ships, 152 National Defense Reserve Fleet ships, 273 U.S. Flag Merchant Marine ships); tactical airlift forces (450 C-130 and about 240 other aircraft); and a large number of logistics support helicopters. In addition, we consider combat equipment in storage depots, located throughout NATO countries, called "POMCUS" (prepositioned material configured in unit sets) to be part of the mobility forces. This is done to facilitate equipment movement and reinforcement planning by having large quantities of supplies and equipment located fairly close to the area where it potentially will be needed.

The mobility forces of the U.S. make a substantial contribution to U.S. national security by allowing us to rapidly reinforce NATO and move forces to meet specific contingencies without dependence upon intermediate bases. Our capabilities in both these areas have been and must be improved in the 1980s, particularly as the number of bases available to us decline through events such as

44

the revolution in Iran. The president has recently proposed some major initiatives in this area as part of the fiscal year 1981 defense budget, and these are most welcome. The proposals will have to be examined carefully, however, and there will undoubtedly be areas where adjustments should be made. But it is a step in the right direction.

ECONOMIC VULNERABILITIES

In the latter part of the twentieth century, any discussion on the subject of national security cannot be limited to talk of guns, tanks, ships, missiles, and airplanes. A new form of warfare must be included in the conversation now, less brutal, maybe, but no less ruthless. The best description for it is "economic warfare."

There is a growing body of literature and, naturally, a large number of theories and schools of thought developing around this concept. It is not really new to the world, but has been more or less "rediscovered," possibly as the horrors of nuclear war have stimulated nations to think of less distasteful or costly or dangerous ways of achieving their objectives.

Americans are no strangers to economic warfare. They have been victims of its battles in recent years, though they probably did not describe it in those terms. I am referring, of course, to the economic pressures resulting from the actions of the cartel formed by the Organization of Petroleum Exporting Countries, or OPEC. If the Soviet Union, either directly or through any of its proxies or client states could gain absolute control of OPEC, it litterally could bring the West to its knees.

Western Europe, even more than the United States, depends on the Persian Gulf region alone for much of its oil imports. The economic disruption and chaos that could follow a complete shutoff of those sources could be devastating. The same is true if, instead of actually gaining control of the OPEC countries, the Soviets were simply able to cut off the sea lanes through which those oil tankers must pass. That would be a powerful combination of both military and economic warfare, taking advantage of both the military and economic weaknesses of the West.

Much the same is true regarding certain strategic minerals that are of vital importance to an industrial society.

The United States—still the strongest economic fortress in the world—must recognze the usefulness of economic power, and must *not be afraid to use* its economic power, in concert with its allies, as a supplement to military power and, in some cases, as an alternative to military power. At the same time, the United States must work to reduce the vulnerabilities of its economy to outside pressures in the same way it must work to reduce its military vulnerabilities.

A WORD ABOUT ARMS LIMITATIONS

Throughout 1979, the subject of strategic arms limitations was discussed and debated, as the president signed and the Senate began the consideration of the SALT II treaty with the Soviet Union. I took an active role in that debate because of my close association with the question of arms control as a member of the Armed Services Committee during 1977 and 1978. At that time, I was a member of the Arms Control Subcommittee, and a Congressional Advisor to the SALT talks.

The SALT II treaty signed by President Carter was a disappointment. Like most Americans, I favor arms control. I have a wife and six children, and I don't want a nuclear holocaust to envelop them or anyone else. But I do not believe that the U.S. should sign an agreement just for the sake of having an agreement. Any arms control treaty must be fair and equitable, it must be verifiable, and it *must truly limit* arms. SALT II, as signed by the president, was none of those things. As this book goes to the printer, the Senate has yet to debate the question of whether to consent to the ratification of SALT II. Obviously, as I write, I cannot predict what the outcome of that debate will be. My hope is that the treaty will be amended to make it an honest and effective arms control agreement, which is equitable and verifiable. If those objectives are not achieved, then it is my belief that *no treaty at all* is better than the treaty as submitted.

One thing can be said with certainty about the debate on SALT II, regardless of whether it is ultimately ratified. That is that the treaty did stimulate the serious consideration by the Congress, by the Administration, and by the general public of the need for increased defense capabilities. The increased fiscal year 1981 defense budget figures I mentioned earlier were a direct outgrowth of that examination of defense needs. I only hope that this newfound concern for an adequate defense is sustained through the amount of time needed to bring new programs and new systems into existence and to get them into the field.

The decade ahead of us will bring new challenges and opportunities to seek the limitation of weapons of mass destruction. If the United States approaches these negotiations from a position of strength, we will be more likely to achieve meaningful limitations and eventual reductions in nuclear arms. We should have learned from our experience with SALT I that the Soviet Union will not go out

47

of its way to abide by the letter or even the spirit of the agreement if it can help it. They have a sorry record of compliance with SALT I, signed in 1972, and the United States must have adequate intelligence capabilities to ensure that the Soviet Union will continue to abide by the terms of the treaty.

A WORD ABOUT INTELLIGENCE CAPABILITIES

Imagine a senior official in the Soviet KGB talking to a member of the U.S. press, saying, ". . . of all the operations that the Soviet Union and the U.S. have conducted against each other, none have benefitted the KGB as much as the campaign in the U.S. to discredit the C.I.A. It's the kind of gift all espionage men dream about. Today our boys have it a lot easier, and we didn't have to lift a finger. You did all our work for us." Incredible as it seems, this quote appeared in *Time* magazine on February 6, 1978, page 10. It may be an exaggeration, but there is no question that the last five years or so haven't been good ones for the Central Intelligence Agency.

The motivations for attacks upon the U.S. intelligence community are mixed. Few have set out intentionally to weaken our national security. But the result has been the same—the credibility of the agencies has been lessened, the morale of many intelligence officers is at rock bottom, and the effectiveness of the intelligence community has been reduced.

Some of the fault for the hazardous seas on which the intelligence agencies find themselves lies with the agencies themselves. In the four years I have sat on the Senate Select Committee on Intelligence, I have seen examples of poor judgment and even illegal actions. Most of these are well-known; they tend to get national headlines, no matter how small or how old the mistakes or the actions were. The point is, the agencies have needed housecleaning. But we must not throw the baby out with the bathwater, to use a well-worn phrase. The reforms that must be made in the intelligence community should be approached carefully and with the single fundamental objective of preserving a strong, capable, and effective intelligence-gathering system.

The reforms should begin with the adoption of *clear legislative charters* for the intelligence agencies. The Charters and Guidelines Subcommittee, on which I serve, is preparing such a charter for the C.I.A., and we will begin the '80s with a more precise definition of the role of intelligence in the formulation of national security policy. Rather than restrict the actions of our intelligence community, clear guidelines will remove the uncertainty that now forces our agencies to choose *not to act,* rather than run the risk of violating someone's measurement of morality or legality.

There are other steps that need to be taken, but I will not take the space to discuss them here. The important thing is to end the "holy war" against the intelligence community and build up our capability to know what we need to know about the world in which we must live and take part as a nation. In an age when massive power can be delivered in a matter of minutes, and when communications can be instantaneous, we cannot afford to have poor intelligence capabilities. There is just no margin for error.

This very brief review of U.S. national security issues can only scratch the surface. But I believe enough has been said to give the reader an idea of the need for substantial changes in the way we go about providing for our national security. We have made some mistakes, but we are in a position to remedy them if we act now in a decisive way. If I can get any message across at all, here, it is that we do in fact face substantial military and economic threats, we are not totally prepared to meet them, and there are things we must do now to defend against them.

The commitment of the American people, in support of elected leaders who share the goal of a strong national defense, is the only true assurance that anything will be done to meet the threats we face as a nation. It is the hope of this chapter to help secure that commitment.

LABOR
PROMOTING FREEDOM
IN THE WORKPLACE

By SENATOR ORRIN HATCH

"In Salt Lake City, Joe," says I,
  Him standing by my bed,
"They framed you on a murder charge"—
Says Joe, "But I ain't dead."
                    —The Ballad of Joe Hill

It is not merely because Salt Lake City is my hometown that I sometimes play *Joe Hill* on the cassette deck I use for listening to taped briefings from my Senate aides while working my way through Washington's commuter traffic. Especially in Paul Robeson's resonant bass version, this story of the immigrant radical labor organizer executed for murder in Utah in 1915 has become one of the noblest folk songs in the language. I have taken a particular delight in it since becoming a member of the Republican minority on the Senate's Labor and Human Resources Committee. All the evidence, after all, is that Joe Hill actually was involved in killing John and Arling Morrison while robbing their grocery store. But you cannot understand the modern American Labor Movement without appreciating the force of myth, particularly for the career bureaucrats who now run most of our large unions.

Take, for example, William W. Winpisinger, president of the International Association of Machinists and Aerospace Workers. Born in 1919, Winpisinger has been with his union continuously since 1947, two years after getting out of the Navy. Now he operates out of offices which, like many labor unions, the IAM has found it necessary to have in a plush area of Washington. Recently he told an interviewer that he was in favor of tax cuts only for "the people that need it . . . and that sure isn't anybody over fifty grand, because I make over fifty grand, and I'll damn well tell you I could pay a lot more taxes and not hurt a bit." (Winpisinger gets $77,000, compared to $60,000 for a U.S. Senator. But that's very low by union standards. Frank Fitzsimmons of the Teamsters gets $156,250.) What hurts Winpisinger a lot, however, is a perfectly normal outbreak of democracy such as Congress's defeat in 1978 of the so-called Labor Law Reform bill. This "reform" would have enormously strengthened the unions' legal powers over workers and managements, without safeguarding against the concomitant problems of corruption, coercion, injustice, and economic inefficiency. These things are the cause of the decline of the American Labor Union Movement. Winpisinger's reaction was extraordinary for a responsible public figure in a free society, especially the United States. "In my lifetime, no group has ever gotten justice in this country without lawlessness," he was quoted as saying in *Time* magazine, September 4, 1978. "So if we want to see change, then we may have to stop having such a high regard for law-and-order." So goes the union movement.

This is not an unrepresentative glance into the Winpisinger world. Speaking at an AFL-CIO conference in August 1978, Winpisinger said of American Conservatives:

Like its spiritual predecessors in Hitler's Germany, Mussolini's Italy, and Franco's Spain, this army of the radical right has nothing but contempt for democracy and democratic institutions. It is diametrically opposed to everything the American labor movement believes in and stands for . . .

That is, what the American labor movement's *leaders* believe in and stand for. In the same speech, Winpisinger denounced Proposition 13, the California initiative that slashed property taxes. He used the standard liberal stance that passage of Proposition 13 was largely due to "fear and hatred of Blacks, Chicanos, the poor and the disadvantaged." But he had to admit:

> In order to carry so overwhelmingly, Proposition 13 had to have wide support among working people. And that included a helluva lot of union members.

Similarly, Winpisinger gave an interview to John D. Lofton Jr., the incisive editor of the American Conservative Union's *Battle Line* magazine. In it, he said that he was a "Democratic Socialist" and that he preferred the economic system of Sweden to that of the United States. Asked whether most union members were Democratic Socialists, Winpisinger replied ominously, "No, not now. But they can be driven there. . . ."

> *Lofton:* I think you're going to have an awful hard time convincing union members that the solution for the economy . . .
>
> *Winpisinger:* Well, let me worry about the hard time. You guys don't worry about it.
>
> *Lofton:* . . . is to centralize it more and make it more state run.
>
> *Winpisinger:* Talking to our members is my job, not yours, thank God.
>
> *Lofton:* We're talking to them too, pal.
>
> *Winpisinger:* You talk to them. If you win 'em . . .
>
> *Lofton:* That's right. And they're listening . . .

53

Winpisinger: If you win 'em, I'll be out of work, and then you'll be happy. (My italics).

Lofton: Oh, no, no. There'll be a good job in the private sector for you.

Winpisinger: I'll see you in hell before you win.

To complete the On The Waterfront image, two unidentified mugs later tried—in August 1978, in broad daylight in a Washington hotel!—to intimidate Lofton into surrendering to them the interview tape.

Winpisinger is obviously unusual, in that he appears to dwell more or less full time in his world of myth and paranoia. But almost all union institutional bureaucrats and their agents are under its fatal spell. The AFL-CIO's Committee of Political Education has circulated a 23-minute film called *The Right Wing Machine* comparing Conservative groups to "rattlesnakes." It is full of such colorful sledgehammer rhetoric that Conservatives have rented it to entertain themselves at private showings. Carl Magel, legislative director of the American Federation of Teachers (!), speaking on the same bill as Winpisinger, told his audience that "the New Right wants to crush labor and control education, which is the way Castro, Franco, Hitler, Mussolini, and Idi Amin all came to power."

Even my esteemed colleague Senator Howard Metzenbaum (D.-Ohio) equated the American Conservative Movement with the anti-Catholic, anti-Semitic "Know-Nothings," and the Ku Klux Klan. When questioned by reporters, however, he kindly declined to place me in that category. ("I wouldn't name any particular senator. Orrin Hatch is a fine fellow and a good friend of mine.")

Even the late AFL-CIO President George Meany, when I introduced myself to him as he sat disconsolately on a couch at a reception shortly after the defeat of Labor Law Reform, sprang upright out of his depression and announced that his movement would spend "whatever it takes" in my next election to be revenged for my leading the opposition in the Senate. He said this in an amicable way. But it is not any politician's idea of pleasant cocktail party chat. And I never got the chance to congratulate him on providing a forum for Russian dissident Alexander Solzhenitsyn when a detente-dazzled Republican president (alas) would not.

You might have thought we had something in common. I am myself a union man. For you see, in 1950 I began work in the construction trades as an apprentice wood, wire, and metal lather, in the AFL-CIO Wood, Wire, and Metal Lather's Union. I became a journeyman lather. I worked with my bare hands for ten years, including two whole years when I had to drop out of law school for lack of funds. I was following in my father's footsteps. He was a union man, and spent his entire working life as a lather in Pittsburgh, Pennsylvania, a quintessential union town. When he was laid off during the Depression, he moved us into a home he built out of lumber from a fire-razed building while he was unemployed.

It's a good feeling to be a union man. It was a good trade, being a lather. I earned considerably more than I did later, when I started out as a lawyer. But it does mean that recently when we came to Washington, I exasperated my wife by complaining incessantly about the workmanship in every new house we thought about buying.

It also means that I can recognize union bluster when I hear it.

What is the reason for the union's hysteria? *Because the union bureaucrats are out of touch with the American worker, and because they are increasingly unsuccessful in influencing the U.S. Congress.* They are literally afraid, as Winpisinger put it in his blundering way, of being "out of work." And they have a lot to lose. Total union income is more than $5.4 billion a year—twice the after-tax income of America's largest industrial corporation, and more than the revenues of 43 states. In America today, unions are big business. Every month, union bureaucrats receive in salaries over $100 million. That is why they try to terrify their members with tales of right-wing ogres. That is why they repeatedly try to get Congress to pass laws to provide the benetfis they cannot negotiate, and why they attempt to force workers who, it is becoming increasingly clear, will never join unions of their own free will to pay dues anyway. And that's why they become increasingly frantic, when these efforts fail.

The figures make this obvious. Union membership has declined as a proportion of the total nonfarm labor force to its lowest point in over forty years. Today, one worker in five is a union member. Unions are winning less than half of the representation elections sanctioned by the National Labor Relations Board. A generation ago, they regularly won two out of three. Even worse, they are losing the right to continue to represent workers in a very high proportion of the increasing number of decertification elections. A Gallup Poll this year found that only 55% of the population approves of unions—the lowest figure in forty years, and a dramatic contrast to the 76% approval rate of 1957, at a time when Congress was

56

actually investigating labor racketeering in a good faith attempt to "keep their act clean."

Even the gains that unions have made are a mixed blessing. They are largely among government workers, whose strikes or "sick-outs" arouse unparalleled public ire.

Labor unions, as we know them today, are largely a creation of politics. In the early Depression union membership had declined to its lowest point for fifteen years, and many authorities thought the movement was dead. It wasn't, because President Roosevelt's New Deal put the force of the federal government behind their efforts to organize workers. Roosevelt confirmed the peculiar legal status of labor unions: as Nobel Prize-winning economist F.A. Hayek has said, they are "uniquely privileged institutions to which the general rules of law do not apply." By 1938, union membership had doubled, and the movement had broken into many fiercely-resisting industries, notably automaking, steel, and rubber.

The labor bosses recognized the source of their good fortune. They set up COPE (the Committee on Political Education) to channel funds to sympathetic political candidates. Now they are redoubling their efforts. In 1978, they gave a record $14 million. In addition, the full-time staffs of labor unions regularly donate their time and resources to selected political campaigns (or rather, the time and resources are paid for by union members). To some extent, the labor unions have been outmaneuvered by their own greed. They supported campaign funding reform, in the expectation that it would eliminate large private contributors, who were assumed to be Conservatives. But they weren't, always—a General Motors heir, Stewart Mott, was the major backer of George McGovern. Furthermore, the new law brought competing forms of finance into politics, in the form of business Political Action Committees, enhanced smaller contributions from the public at large, or of matching federal funds.

As we enter the decade of the 1980s, the union bosses aren't getting everything they want from Congress anymore. Nor are employers caving in at the mere presence at the worksite. They can still win defensive battles—maintaining the minimum wage laws, or preventing reform of other outmoded wage laws like the Davis-Bacon Act, which gives labor unions a stranglehold over federal construction projects. But those of us who oppose these power grabs have been increasingly able to deny them the new privileges they are counting on to go forward into the 1980s. In spite of a Democratic Congress and Administration in the 95th Congress, labor unions did not get the Common Situs Picketing Bill, which would have given any one union the power to close down construction sites, the Cargo Preference Bill, which was effectively a subsidy to maritime unions, the original Humphrey-Hawkins Bill, which would have confirmed government control over the economy, the Consumer Protection Agency, and above all the so-called Labor Law Reform Bill.

Union bureaucrats like Mr. Winpisinger are delicate plants. They need the sun of federal favor so they can blossom and fill the air with their fragrance. Any sign of a shadow, and they start to wave their tendrils desperately. That's what's going on today.

This division between the union leaders and their members arises out of irrepressible sociological conflict. Blue collar workers, particularly the skilled, have done well in American society. Many of them earn more than white collar workers, just as I did when I became a fully-qualified lather. They are responsible members of the middle class. They are the backbone of this country. And in America, it is the middle class who pay the taxes.

Union leaders know by now that their members don't like paying taxes. Political defeats for union bosses like Proposition 13 in 1978, and 1979's Proposition 4—which limited the Californina state government's expenditures—have made that clear. The union leaders' solution is traditional: tax the rich more.

But this isn't a solution in America. There just aren't that many rich—or even upper-income earners. The structure of income distribution in the United States is not really a pyramid. It's more like a pancake with a needle stuck in its centre. The vast majority of Americans are in the pancake, earn very close to the average wage. Only a few earn even twice that: the numbers earning significantly higher are minute. It has been calculated that if you confiscated the entire income of those earning above $200,000—chopped off the point of the needle—it would run the government for only two weeks.

It is arithmetically impossible for the government to spend over 40% of our Gross National Product, as it is now doing, without taxing most people significantly. Washington tries to do it indirectly, by taxing "corporate earnings and by inventing things like the "windfall profits tax" to commandeer the effects of any major shifts in commodity prices that might occur. This distorts the economy by preventing price signals from getting through to and telling investors where to put their capital. It is ultimately self-defeating. It just means higher prices and fewer jobs. There is no way around the problem. Everyone has to pay.

The union bureaucrats themselves, however, are not personally sensitive to this problem. For one thing, they earn much more than their members. They aren't feeling the financial pain of Middle Americans trying to educate their children while making ends meet. Secondly, the bureaucrats are themselves closely linked to the army of government administrators, regulators, planners, analysts, and plain paper-shufflers that has been expanding in America ever since the 1930s. These are the people who are paid by the taxpayers, union and nonunion, in order to supervise redistribution programs, in alliance with their sympathizers in many universities and the media. Sociologists call these people the "New Class." They have no direct contact with productive enterprise. Their position in society is dependent upon the power and expansion of government. Accordingly, they tend to favor the advance of government power into American life at every opportunity—energy, environment, safety on the job—until finally they are advocating political control of the entire economy.

One case of the growth and abuse of government power in the labor area is the Occupational Safety and Health Act story.

When Congress passed the Occupational Safety and Health Act of 1970, it unfortunately cast the government in the role of policeman to enforce occupational safety and health in more than four million workplaces in the United States. This scheme has not produced demonstrable improvements in the safety of workers. Injury data indicate that, since OSHA began, there has been a modest 11% reduction in the number of injuries, despite the *billions* of dollars spent on OSHA programs. However, injuries which result in lost workdays—the more serious incidents—are up 19%. Although these data are not conclusive, because they are influenced by factors such as improved workers' compensation and economic recession, it is indisputable that the act has not been an overwhelming success.

What has been successful through OSHA is the creation of a large bureaucracy within the Department of Labor, and further opportunity for big labor to control governmental labor policy. Unfortunately, labor's historical adversary relationship with the private sector promotes ideas like OSHA, and is counter-productive to facilitating self-initiative in the workplace to improve occupational safety and health.

But there is no clearer or more important example of the conflict between the interests of union members and the interests of the union bureaucrats than so-called Affirmative Action. It may not be too surprising that labor union leaders were prepared to acquiesce in what is, in fact, the most radical assault upon the principles of equal protection and of liberty since our Republic was founded. Affirmative Action has been advanced covertly and in the name of the unchallengeable cause of civil rights. But union leaders' outright betrayal of the American worker —particularly the white male, who will be directly and grievously and unfairly injured by Affirmative Action— is astonishing to me. It is further evidence of the extent to which the bureaucracies that now run America's labor unions have been co-opted by their allies in the government process.

The story is briefly this. The 1964 Civil Rights Act prohibited discrimination by race across a wide area of American life. No sooner was it law, however, than the federal bureaucracy began to pressure business, educational, and government institutions to do exactly that— to discriminate *in favor* of minorities. By the end of the 1970s, the federal bureaucracy was effectively requiring quotas for an ever-increasing number of officially-recognized "minorities." (The handicapped and "Spanish-surnamed" Americans are minorities; Polish, Jewish Americans, etc., are not.)

This is contrary to the wording of the Civil Rights Act. It conflicts with repeated assurances given by the Senate floor managers at the time Congress passed the act—normally a key factor in the resolution of disputes over the meaning of legislation. Furthermore, I believe it is unconstitutional. But in the 14 years between the passage of the Civil Rights Act and the Supreme Court's *Bakke* decision, powerful interests in the federal bureaucracy and the private sector had flourished under Affirmative Action, both through enforcing it and/or benefiting from it. A whole class would be overthrown if its illegality were exposed, not something the Supreme Court approaches lightly. On the other hand, if the Supreme Court were to uphold Affirmative Action and its often conflicting requirements, it would be effectively legislating for racial quotas supported by massive government intervention throughout American life. This is not envisaged nor allowed for in the Constitution. It is at variance with America's political culture. And it would represent a breach of the separation of powers.

The Supreme Court is still wrestling with the issue as we enter the 1980s. The results to date appear to be an example of class justice. Quotas were struck down as illegal in the case of Alan Bakke, a student who had been excluded from medical school because of them, and he was admitted. They were upheld in the case of Brian Weber, a refinery worker, who had been prevented from entering a training program to which his seniority entitled him, and he was excluded. I disagree with the arguments of the majority in the *Weber* case. As a lawyer, I find no basis in law for the distinction between the two. It is

62

impossible to avoid the feeling that some commentators who supported the Supreme Court's decision in the *Weber* case simply don't expect that their children will want to work at craft jobs in Louisiana oil refineries.

But the majority of Americans want and need those jobs, and their white collar equivalents. They don't want to see blacks or anybody else excluded from all the possibilities that America has to offer. At the same time, they don't want or deserve to be confined into an ever-narrowing area of opportunity themselves. Nonetheless, large labor union's were not at the forefront defending the rights of refinery worker Brian Weber. The AFL-CIO even submitted a brief to the Supreme Court *against* Mr. Weber.

There is a further reason why the labor unions are losing touch with their membership. It relates to the economic impact of unions. Labor unions simply have had little impact upon the wage rates of their members. And workers are beginning to realize this.

From an economic point of view, labor is a commodity, and wages are the price of that commodity. According to the propaganda of the unions, employers will grind that price down as low as they can. Only the workers' solidarity stands between them and a permanent diet of bread and cheese. But this *is not true*. If wages are low, and employers are making high profits, other employers will move in, increasing the demand for labor. Employers will bid against each other for workers, and wages will move up. Conversely, if the employers are not making money, and if the workers strike to obtain higher wages, the employers will simply fold.

In a vast economy like that of the United States, it is impossible to suppress, indefinitely, the effects of supply and demand. The most the labor unions can do is to act as a cartel, artificially exaggerating the price of labor at one point in the system, at the expense of some other point. To do this, they must have legal immunities and government support, otherwise they will be undercut by market forces. Thus, for example, labor unions have insisted on a series of minimum wage laws. While this may benefit workers who actually have jobs, it means that many marginal employers will not hire extra workers.

The real victims are the unemployed. They are the youth, and particularly the 35-40% poor black youth who have been priced *out of the market* by the same union movement that is pledged to secure "economic opportunity for all." They are unable to get work by accepting lower remuneration, as would normally happen, because it is illegal for employers to pay it to them. The minimum wage laws also make it economic for employers to automate earlier, since they cannot substitute cheap labor. This further cuts the number of jobs. The same process is in operation at every level in the economic system, wherever labor unions fix the rate for a job.

A recent Library of Congress study quoted labor economists as tentatively estimating the difference between union and nonunion wages in selected industries at 5-15%. (They were tentative because of awkward methodological problems. For example, one new study suggests it is *not* that unions cause higher wages, but that high-wage workers tend to join unions). This is not much for all the fuss, particularly when union dues run into hundreds of dollars a year for each union worker.

Employers often resist unions fiercely, generally not because they are afraid of high wages but of lack of flexibility. Union organizers cost employers time in lengthy negotiating, in job disputes with other unions, and so on.

Organizers sometimes show signs of preferring to have large numbers of workers in low-paying jobs but dependent upon the union, rather than an independent few in higher-paying jobs, even if the increased efficiency would open up opportunities for the rest elsewhere. Politically-motivated organizers can totally cripple industries while bringing their loyal but credulous members no tangible benefit at all.

This point is equally true for the economy at large. Even where empirical studies seem to show that organized labor earns more, the distortion that the union is causing in the economy will result in misallocation of resources and a diminution of overall welfare. The earnings of some other nonunion group may well be depressed, and even the union members might earn more if they abandoned their union demands and let the system work. The evidence seems to be that many younger workers simply don't want to join unions in the first place.

I am not one of those who think labor unions can be dispensed with altogether. They are as useful as any other community organization. The freedom to organize *is an intrinsic part* of our overall freedoms. It is a guarantee to the worker against management abuse in the last resort. It is obvious that even nonunionized employers think more carefully about the way they treat their employes because there are unions abroad in the land. The IBM Corporation is a classical example of what I am referring to. IBM, with 325,000 employees in 23 U.S. plants, have managed to remain nonunion because of lavish benefits, good pay, few layoffs, and a strong emphasis on good personnel policies. All without union intervention.

But it is equally obvious that there is great potential for union abuse of their own members, employers, and the American public. Anyone who reads the press can see that there is still a constant undertone of violence, corruption, and intimidation in America's labor unions.

In the 1980s, it seems to me, the watchword for real labor law reform must be "freedom"—both as an ideal and as a method of operation.

That is why I introduced into both the 95th and 96th Congress the Employee Freedom of Representation Bill, which is essentially an equitable National Right To Work Act. The principle of voluntary association, guaranteed in the First Amendment, was a central tenet in the policy of union pioneer Samuel Gompers, and it was included in the original National Labor Relations Act. Unfortunately, the principle has slipped. Today, when a union gets 51% of a representation election in most states, *all* the workers can be compelled to join and are subject to its discipline. This simply puts too much power in the union officials' hands, both in relation to the employer and in relation to the employe, especially where exclusive hiring hall agreements are the practice.

I am not insensitive to the unions' arguments that compulsory unionism eliminates the "free rider," the non-union worker who receives the fruits of the unions's efforts without paying dues. Accordingly, my bill would also relieve unions of their current legal obligation to bargain for or otherwise represent employes who decline to join or financially support the union.

This bill would not cripple unions. Unions would earn the support of their members through effective representation.

In a similar vein, I have introduced bills which I hope will become law in the 1980s that would allow skilled tradesmen to form their own unions by being able to opt out of the industrial unions to which the National Labor Relations Board has effectively assigned them, to allow those with religious objections to opt out of unions provided they donate to charity the equivalent of their dues, and pay the costs where the union is forced by law to act in their behalf.

There are a number of specific legal restrictions that unions cling to which are antisocial and should be swept away in the 1980s. The most notorious is the Davis-Bacon Act, which according to the General Accounting Office adds about $2.7 billion in unnecessary construction costs annually, and benefits only a small group of construction workers. It is a "taxpayer rip-off" of the highest order.

In 1979, I introduced bills designed to increase youth employment by relaxing the stranglehold of the minimum wage. Furthermore I have introduced a Freedom from Quotas Act, which is intended to reassert the principle of freedom in the workplace. It would end quotas that punish ordinary Americans by allowing discrimination. But this is an issue which reaches beyond the area of labor practices, and into the spirit of the Constitution itself.

These positive proposals are not received well by the liberal Democratic majority in Congress. In the decade of the 1980s, however, conservative Americans must constantly assert the truth about labor relations inside Congress if it is to prevail outside. That is the starting point for the changes which must be made in the next decade, if our free enterprise system will prosper, nurturing with it the well-being of our labor movement.

The primary goals of our National Labor Policy in

the 1980s must be government neutrality, the preservation of our free collective bargaining system, and guaranteeing employe freedom of choice.

It is important to the success and prosperity of business, and the prosperity of workers that the economy go forward in an atmosphere of mutual respect and understanding. Employes should have the right to organize and to bargain collectively through union representatives, or to refrain from doing so, through secret ballot elections. In the 1980s we need a balance in labor-management relations. *Freedom of choice is fundamental* in maintaining this critical balance. Our current laws which provide special privileges and immunities for labor—such as exemption from antitrust laws—will have to be reexamined to determine whether they undermine employe free choice. While most Americans have no antiunion animus, they want a reduction of big labor union power.

It is time that American labor policy reflected the will of our citizens—the organized and unorganized. For far too long the basic issues of management and labor have been removed from the context of the marketplace, and been dealt with in a maze of government interference and regulation. This is largely due to labor's rigid faith in big government programs as the solution to all worker problems. The *single most vital need* of our economy is growth and investment in the private sector, and a commensurate decline in public sector involvement. Such a course will benefit American business, by freeing it from duplicative regulations and laws that have stunted and stagnated economic growth. By creating greater opportunity and prosperity, it will also greatly benefit the American worker. Far too much damage has been done to our economy by artificial arrangements that reflect neither the true strengths of the workforce nor the best social arrangements. Government has dictated wage rates, and has encouraged policies that are duplicative and inflationary.

In the 1980s America's labor needs call for training minorities—absent quotas—to compete with all other members of the workforce, and for the payment of fair and well-deserved wages. But we must learn to attain these goals at a pace our economy can absorb, and through the economic planning of a private sector that is free from restraints to work together with labor. An economy that is free from such restraints will be a far more productive one, and that will benefit every worker.

There *is* a place in labor-management relations for government involvement. Under certain circumstances it is necessary. But it must survive only in a framework of impartiality circumscribed by fairness.

I look towards a future in the 1980s where management and labor, on an equal footing, are free to resolve their disputes through an open exchange of policies and ideas, without the intervention of government on either side. We should seek to give true meaning to the philosophy of the First Amendment, which suggests that all people can exchange ideas and, without coercion, seek to convert others to their ideals. Only in this atmosphere shall the strength of ideas govern the future of our laboring society.

I'll end with another of my favorite folk songs, the story of "John Henry," whose job was laying railroad track, and who found himself confronted with a steam drill that could allegedly do his job faster. The song has John Henry challenging the machine to a race, with the words

A man ain't nothing but a man.
But before I let that steam drill beat me down, Lord, lord,
I'll die with my hammer in my hand.

What "John Henry" celebrates is the profound conservatism, respect for individual dignity, and approbation of a job for its own sake that characterizes the American working class.

And that is why I am confident that the cause of conservatism will ultimately triumph among America's workers. For it is their own.

FOREIGN POLICY
FACING REALITY IN THE '80s

By SENATOR PAUL LAXALT

We Americans tend to see ourselves in two rather different lights. On the one hand, we are a pragmatic "can-do" people. On the other, we are highly idealistic, holding firmly to certain fundamental beliefs for which we consider ourselves torchbearers to the rest of the world.

As I see it, a successful American foreign policy must adequately reflect both these two basic facets of the American character. It must be pragmatic in dealing with the world as it is. Yet it must also be idealistic in pursuit of goals which are worthy of the American people. Neither facet is sufficient without the other. Idealism without attention to power realities degenerates into empty moral posturing. Pure pragmatism for its own sake becomes cynically self-serving.

Perhaps in reaction to Vietnam and Watergate, American power in recent years has emphasized the idealistic to the neglect of essential power realities. Accordingly, as I see it, the agenda for the 1980s has to be *to restore the balance*. Principally, this means coming to grips with the fact of continued, powerful, and implacable opposition from the Soviet Union. It is necessary that we do this not just for our national survival—although this is certainly reason enough. It is equally important that we do so if we are to have any chance at all of promoting those basic principles which all Americans hold dear and which we all wish to see survive and flourish.

Both idealism and pragmatism in foreign policy are deeply embedded in the American past. Stretching back to the Constitutional Convention and even before, there have been Americans who argued that the United States needed to come to grips with the world as it is, as well as those who maintained that, owing to our unique geographical and historical position, we could do without the sordid power politics of Europe and build a society which, by force of example, would bring home certain basic truths to the rest of the world.

In the 19th century, the debate tended to be focused on the question of U.S. involvement in the affairs of the European powers. Idealists tended to be isolationists arguing that the United States, along the lines of Washington's *Farewell Address,* would do better to avoid "entangling alliances." The pragmatists, on the other hand, argued that the balance of power in Europe, if swayed too far in the direction of a single power, could also prejudice American security. Owing to the absence of such an all-powerful conqueror and the presence of the British fleet, the isolationists usually got the better of the argument at that time.

By World War I, American idealism had taken a slightly different hue. While idealists still wished to avoid sordid, entangling alliances, it was clear that the security of the United States was intimately bound up with the fate of Europe, East Asia, and elsewhere. Thus was born the kind of crusading idealism which has been dubbed Wilsonianism. The force of the American example was now to be backed by American military might. And while President Wilson himself certainly wished that the United States would continue to act as a major player on the world stage, the idea of first making the world safe for democracy and then retreating from the problems left by the war was politically just too tempting. So the United States again retreated within itself, a move which helped to set the stage for another and still more destructive war.

A better balance between idealism and power politics was struck after World War II. To many analysts, these were the glory days of American foreign policy. American military might ruled supreme. Over Soviet opposition, our principles of human rights, self-determination, and national sovereignty were implanted in the new international order. Although this is now coming apart, it has stood the world in good stead for better than a quarter of a century.

Vietnam *marked the end* of this postwar period. Certainly it came as a traumatic shock to the foreign policy establishment. Ricocheting from what was seen as a crusade against Soviet power, they preached that the United States had no further need to contain the Soviets, because the Cold War was over, and because more important issues were coming to the fore.

The Soviet Union was portrayed as a country beset by significant internal problems with an aged leadership concerned only with the status quo. Conflicts between the two major powers were based largely on misunderstanding which, with a little patience and good will, could be resolved. Progress towards liberalization within the Soviet Union was inevitable, and the United States needed only to be conciliatory in order to placate certain unspecified "doves" within the Kremlin to insure peace between the superpowers.

Needless to say, Soviet tanks in Afghanistan have now dissipated a good deal of this wishful thinking. Certainly this event was most disturbing, in that a *direct invasion* by Soviet troops of a country not usually thought part of their "bloc" marks a new level of aggressiveness. Still it is surprising that, in a decade perhaps most strikingly characterized by Soviet adventurism by Cuban proxy, it has taken so long and such a dramatic event to dispel our delusions about passivity and inaction acting as a substitute for firm policy.

In November of 1978, as part of a delegation of senators, I visited the Kremlin and met with Soviet leaders, including Brezhnev and Kosygin. It was plain to me then that these people were tough, resourceful, and implacable adversaries. Far from being paunchy, status quo oriented bureaucrats, they were ruthless antagonists, I recognized immediately, just waiting for a chance to take what they wanted.

Yet for some reason, throughout the decade of the 1970s, under Democratic and Republican Administrations alike, the United States seemed unwilling or unable to come to grips with this basic fact. Instead, our interests have been elsewhere. After Vietnam, the 1970s became the decade of detente, arms control, and human rights. All of these are legitimate, and some pressing concerns. But in focusing upon them, we have taken our eyes off the essential dilemma associated with the massive buildup of Soviet military might occurring at the same time.

In the spring of 1978, I was the floor leader in opposition to the Panama Canal Treaties. As I saw it, then, the proposal to give away the Canal was quite simply a proposal to relinquish a major strategic asset to a highly unreliable partner in exchange for paper promises of future use. I was told by the Administration and the State

Department that the reason for this was to improve our image in Latin America. Yet, there was a studied unwillingness to consider Torrijo's relationship with Castro and the Soviets, an absolute repudiation of any possibility that the Panamanian dictator would seek to foment revolution in other Central American countries, and fervent expressions of hope that I would give up my "cold warrior" mentality.

After the Sandinista revolution in Nicaragua, I think we can all see the danger in this kind of thinking. While it is true that not every stirring in the world can be interpreted as a direct function of Soviet-American conflict, it is also true that, unless we are firm in maintaining that balance, we will find our basic principles as well as our position in the world slipping.

Detente in the 1970s has been mostly sham from the beginning. Playing upon our people's heartfelt desire for peace, the Soviets in the 1970s have spoken the language of peace, coexistence, and reconciliation of differences while aggressively pursuing their designs in the Third World and elsewhere.

In the wake of the Soviet invasion of Afghanistan, analysts and commentators in this country are now discussing whether we are seeing a reversion to the bad old days of the Cold War. "Is this Cold War II?" they ask.

In fact, the Cold War never ended. It didn't even slow down. The principal difference between the so-called decade of detent in the 1970s and the Cold War of earlier years was our refusal to read Soviet actions for what they really were. We preferred to interpret them *as we wished them to be.*

Indeed, as Eugene Rostow has argued in an authoritative *Commentary* article in February 1979, the 1970s marked a new high watermark of Soviet aggressiveness.

As he put it, ". . . the Interim Agreement (SALT I) has been an important structural feature of the most turbulent and dangerous period of the Cold War, the period ironically known as detente."

Human rights has proven almost equally hollow. Concern for the individual liberties of the citizens of other lands is a long-standing, legitimate objective of U.S. foreign policy. But our focus on empty rhetoric in cases where we have very little leverage, has helped neither our overall image nor the unfortunate victims of human rights violations overseas.

What should we do about individual liberties in states —such as the Soviet Union—that are militarily powerful, economically largely independent, and utterly oppressive of the individual rights of their citizens? I admit this is a serious question for which I have no ready answer. However, I can say what I think we should *not* do: we should not cast off our friends in the name of moral standards which, fairly applied, condemn our enemies far more strongly.

In addition, as a responsible government, the United States should not indulge in empty posturing. Warnings, admonitions, and even threats emanating from Washington *need to be seen* to carry weight. Too often in the last decade they simply have not.

Clearly, we are unable to do much about the flagrant abuses of human rights in the Soviet Union and the People's Republic of China. Clearly, we have much greater influence with those countries that are smaller and are closer to us. The result has been a kind of selective morality in which we punish those small countries which would like to be friendly to us by holding them up to an abstract standard of human rights morality, and absolve those powerful countries who are our adversaries because we have little leverage over them.

Another offshoot of the failure in Vietnam has to do with what might be called the myth of the guerrilla. Left-wing students and part of the media in this country tended to glorify the Vietcong and the North Vietnamese. Because these people ultimately defeated the mighty American military establishment, a myth grew out that they were somehow romantic and heroic. Related to this, established governments which oppose these heroes and romantics were painted as repressive and reactionary.

Both our human rights standards and our glorification of terrorists and guerrillas have established standards of purity which real life governments who would like to be our friends stood no chance of meeting. They have also been selectively applied. There has been no assessment of the track record of Marxist governments once they are in power. And these standards applied to existing governments have been so impossibly ideal as to insure that they would inevitably come up short.

In November of 1976, as part of a delegation of senators which visited the Middle East, I had occasion to meet with the Shah of Iran. Even then, he was convinced that, should he get into trouble, the United States could not be relied upon to provide effective support. His reasoning was complex. But there was no question that our recent focus on excessive moral purity was a major factor in his thinking.

Americans historically have not been fond of intricate power balances. They have reeked too much of sordid backroom deals by European cabinets. We have liked to consider ourselves above such things, and preferred to operate on the basis of certain universal principles.

But now we have no choice. The United States is a fundamental part of any balance of power vis-à-vis the Soviet Union. With the democratic world obviously under siege, American power is indispensable. As I see it, the decade of the 1980s must be a reawakening to these fundamental principles.

Such a reawakening requires both the will and the wherewithal to face down the Soviet challenge. There is now a clear need for a precise definition of what our national interests are and where our priorities lie. It is critically important that we begin immediately to confront geopolitical thrusts by the Soviet Union in such areas as Iran and Afghanistan.

Politically, this will be difficult, in that the Soviets are quite astute. Many of their probings will be made in relatively marginal areas where it will be difficult for us to mobilize a political consensus, particularly if the Soviets periodically back off and launch so-called peace offensives.

In the 1950s, this approach was characterized as "salami tactics," and it will be imperative in the next decade to develop policy for dealing with these threats, at the margin accompanied by post-hoc protestations of friendship, or be faced by their continuing, successful application.

In my trip to the Soviet Union, it was clear just how effective such Russian tactics can, be. One issue at that time concerned the stationing of MIG-23s in Cuba. In terms of this overall strategic balance, the relatively small

78

number of fighter aircraft involved would not be decisive. But still, the stationing of nuclear-capable aircraft in Cuba clearly violated the understanding reached between President Kennedy and Nikita Khrushchev, as well as its subsequent updating.

It was clear that, if left in place, the MIGs would be a harbinger of things to come. A confrontation between Premier Kosygin and a number of senators grew very heated. Unfortunately, President Carter later chose to let the incident pass over. As a result, attack submarines and combat troops, in addition to the MIG-23s, are now involved in the construction of what Senator Jackson has appropriately called "fortress Cuba."

For the 1980s, an effective foreign policy will require an awareness of the danger of such tactics, and a willingness to resist them. It will also require the wherewithal to be employed in maintaining necessary power balances. Senator Garn has discussed the question of a rearmament of our basic capabilities, elsewhere in this book. I certainly concur with him that it is vitally important to rebuild both our strategic forces *and* our general purpose forces.

Senator McClure has discussed our energy needs in another chapter. Certainly an effective foreign policy for the 1980s requires adequate supplies of energy. This means not only maximum utilization of available domestic sources to reduce our reliance on unstable foreign sources, but also a firm resolve to face down the growing Soviet threat to the Persian Gulf states, to insure that our access—and that of our allies—to necessary Gulf oil supplies is not precipitously cut off.

The Greek Historian Thucydides encapsulated our basic dilemma for the 1980s as well as anyone when he said:

> In human disputation justice is only agreed on when the necessity is equal; whereas they that have the odds of power exact as much as they can, and the weak yield to such conditions as they can get.

There is no need for the 1980s necessarily to be a time of doom and gloom. As our delusions were largely self-inflicted, so we can lift ourselves from them, *if we only muster the will* to do so.

The Soviets—with a failing economy, disastrous agricultural problems, and their own share of social and ethnic problems, to say nothing of the coming leadership crisis—are hardly supermen. In comparison, the United States and its NATO allies have three times the GNP, four times the population, and a far more technologically advanced society.

If we do what is necessary, the odds are clearly in our favor for the 1980s. We can control our own destiny in the next decade. It is for us to decide.

As I see it, the United States is in the world as a major actor, whether we wish to acknowledge it or not. As such, we must learn the basic rules of sound policy and understand that certain laws of power reality obtain, irrespective of our wishes. Once we do so, and adequately reassert American power in the world, then can we both sustain our national security and support those basic principles which have made our nation a beacon for the rest of the world. Then we will truly have what President Carter has promised: a foreign policy as good as our people.

ENERGY
A POSITIVE APPROACH

By SENATOR JAMES A. McCLURE

Jarred awake by the alarm clock beside him, John threw back the heavy covers. The cold air from the floor hit him and, as he groped for his slippers, he remembered the good days of electric blankets, warm rooms, and comfort —the days before the government-decreed thermostat settings of 58°F during the day and 50°F at night.

Then he remembered the inspector's visit, and the $50 fine he had recently paid for leaving the thermostat "just a little higher." His children had been having colds, and it seemed justified, but the inspector said "No." So now they would have to wait another month to purchase new tires for the car. They didn't drive much now, anyway.

Breakfast, instead of constituting a pleasant start for the day, was rushed, in anticipation of the relatively warm ride in the city bus. As John shaved, his thoughts turned to the union meeting scheduled for that evening; it would be the start of a push for higher wages to help meet the steadily increasing fuel and energy bills. But in this year of 1999 John's employer, Ford Motor, was not competitive with foreign car manufacturers: higher wages could result in the Big Two becoming the Big One—GM — which would be disastrous for John. In addition to his wife and two children, John was supporting his brother-in-law, who had lost his job when the aluminum company he worked for had closed down due to energy costs, and his uncle, whose employer—a steel company—had moved overseas in order to obtain a reliable energy supply. Both Canada and Mexico, John recalled, had been making Ford offers of abundant, relatively cheap fuel and electricity.

As he hurried, John wondered about the radio report on how well people were living in other countries. Places like France, for example, where exports were booming, and the standard of living had decreased by only 3% during the past year. Of course, the French *could* be competitive in foreign markets, because of their lower energy costs. The massive French nuclear energy program had resulted not only in conventional power reactors, with the nuclear fuel enrichment and reprocessing plants required to keep them operating, but also in a breeder-reactor program that would enable the French to complete their research and development programs leading to atomic fusion, solar power, and other virtually inexhaustible energy sources. The last such program in the U.S. had been dropped last year: the energy required to operate it had become needed elsewhere. Now, in every American industrial city, the skies were growing darker, as the nation's pollution-control equipment was being shut down to conserve energy. America's critically-needed oil wells were shutting down more frequently, too, as fuel—even for drilling equipment—became more scarce. As for the large hydroelectric projects begun in the 1980s, a lack of fuel had brought construction to a stop there as well: energy alternatives could not be developed without energy.

As John waited for the bus, he watched the traffic

jam of bicycles and foreign cars. Bitterly, he asked himself, "Why didn't someone warn me it would be like this?"

That is the purpose of this chapter: to warn the American people of the consequences of our government's present energy policies. If the antienergy attitude of the present Administration and Congress is not replaced with a positive, forward-looking philosophy, the fictional John will become a widespread reality in American society.

But that negative attitude most certainly can be replaced. It will require, however, a *new awareness* on the part of the people: an awareness that they have been deceived with respect to the energy problem by certain groups. Americans have been told that the energy crisis was not real, that it would "disappear if new federal bureaucracies, such as the Department of Energy, were established. Americans have also been told that producing energy would destroy our natural environment and slowly poison us to death. After that nonsense was dispelled, the story was told that the only way to get around the government roadblocks preventing energy development was to make the federal government (!) the major developer of energy. In case that should happen, those familiar with the way the government operates the Post Office and the railroads are already starting to buy warm clothes and bicycles.

Today there is a cycle of increased government controls which *create* energy shortages, thereby creating more government controls, thereby creating more shortages, and on and on. This cycle can be broken. In the 1980s the United States once again can have control over its energy sources. The United States *does not* have to be subjected to energy shortages due to revolutions or changes in governments overseas, or decisions by foreign oil producers to reduce exports.

The first step in revitalizing our national energy program in the 1980s is to recognize that the present energy policies are not accidental or haphazard. These policies are developed by people motivated by a sincere, dedicated belief in the philosophy that our own energy resources must not be expanded. Who are these antienergy advocates?

Tom Wolfe has called them the "me generation," and Herman Kahn terms them the "new class." They sometimes *pose* as consumerists or environmentalists, thereby bringing criticism upon people legitimately working to protect consumers and the environment. Whatever their label, however, this group is an affluent, politically active, articulate minority whose influence is felt far out of proportion to its numbers. This is partly because the members of this group often occupy key positions in the media and in federal agencies, through which they can act to publicize and further their beliefs. The philosophy definitely is not shared by the normal working American, who is not represented in their numerous committees, institutes, and organizations dedicated to the control of new energy forms.

First and foremost, the advocates of this "new-class" philosophy want to limit economic growth. This is ironic because they are the beneficiaries of America's past growth. Having reaped the benefits of an expansionary economy, they are beginning to question the merit of further expansion. This is because they see such expansion as infringing on their ability to enjoy the material benefits they now have.

Another characteristic of the new class is that, while giving lip service to the concept of democracy, it actually disregards it. Nowhere was this more dramatically demonstrated than in the recent California Initiatives related to a Nuclear Moratorium. The citizens of California voted by a margin of more than two-to-one *against* such a moratorium, and yet the state bureaucrats turned around and imposed one anyway. (So much for the popular will.) These people honestly *believe that they know better* than the rest of society. They see themselves as more insightful, intelligent, and perceptive than the rest of the population, and feel that this gives them the right to impose their standards and their values on the remainder of society.

On the surface, what the new class is advocating is a return to a simpler, less hectic existence. On the surface it is certainly attractive. It is a pastoral vision, out of late 19th century England, with every man a country squire. The only problem is that, during this period, every man is not a squire. The new-class vision bears no resemblance to the society that would result from the policies they advocate. Their society, which they term a stable state economy, would be more akin to the feudal era than to the last period of the Industrial Revolution.

The advocates of the "stable state economy" realize that if you can control the supply of energy, you control the rate of economic growth. Energy is the one crucial variable in any economic system. No matter how high the cost of energy, a way can be found to pay for it. This lesson has been learned well in both Europe and Japan, which experience far higher energy costs than does the United States. In the case of both, economic adjustments have been made, and methods of conservation have been instituted.

On the other hand, if energy is not available, nothing can make up for its absence. Consequently, control of the supply of energy is tantamount to control of the economy. This, in turn, would give the federal government an unprecedented ability to control individual lifestyles.

The desire to control the behavior of the energy-using population, or to control behavior generally, is found throughout the actions proposed by the new class.

The key lies in *attitude*. As I mentioned earlier, members of the new class sincerely believe they are wiser than we are, and that their superior knowledge gives them the right to impose their standards, values, and lifestyles on the rest of us, regardless of our wishes. After all, it's for our own good.

This relentless onslaught seems to be progressing on all fronts. Virtually every energy option is under attack. First, nuclear plants came under fire. Opponents of the atom claimed that anyone advocating nuclear power or connected with it in any fashion was committing random, willful murder. Shortly thereafter, coal came under attack. Persons advocating coal as a fuel were charged with being polluters who were going to raise the earth's CO_2 level to the point that the polar icecaps would melt. (Even that benign source of electricity, hydroelectric power, is suspect. There always seems to be an endangered species somewhere near the site of a proposed dam, and no matter how far along the project is, the Endangered Species Act is used to stop it.)

Solar energy appears to be an acceptable alternative until you start talking about providing it in large amounts. Then, problems with capital costs and land use arise. The one common factor shared by the opponents of all these various energy forms is that, as long as a particular energy program remains unfeasible, or in the planning stage, it is all right, but the moment it seems that the option may become practical, it is met with opposition.

On the surface the picture is bleak; there is, however, some good as well as some bad news. The bad news is that, at present, the opponents of a secure energy future seem to have the initiative. The good news is that the initiative *can* be taken back. America has a number of advantages which can be capitalized on in the 1980s. First, the public does not want our country to stand still: virtually every poll taken regarding energy attitudes has demonstrated that most Americans favor the development of *all* energy options, whether they be coal, nuclear energy, or some other energy forms.

Secondly, *the facts support energy development.* The opponents of the development of our domestic energy supplies have relied for too long on excessive rhetoric and emotion to carry their message. They simply do not have their facts straight. For the most part their inaccuracies are so blatant that even the unsophisticated observer can see through them when challenged by accurate data.

A third point is that the American public is basically optimistic. People want to believe that we can solve our problems, and are rapidly tiring of those harbingers of doom who see disaster in every positive action.

It is essential that we solve our problems to ensure that our children and grandchildren will continue to enjoy the standard of living and personal freedom which our economic system has created.

The second step follows logically from the first: to recognize that the antienergy philosophy is basically immoral. The advocates for energy security must, therefore, recognize that *their position is the moral one*. In the historical battle between the individual versus government control, the antienergy advocates are on the side of the government.

That philosophy directly threatens our energy security, thereby threatening our economy, our national defense, and, indeed, our social and political system. We dare not underestimate the seriousness of drastic, long-term reductions in energy supply. The brief crises of 1973-74 and in early 1979 were just quick tastes of what life could be like if the opponents of energy growth continue to win their battles in the 1980s.

Nuclear energy provides a classic example of the antienergy movement in action. While energy in general is under attack, it is the antinuclear movement that is the largest and most active. It operates on both a national and international scale. For that reason alone a thorough airing of the nuclear issue would be in order. But there is also the reality that the days of fossil fuels are numbered. Oil and natural gas already are too valuable as feedstocks to be used as fuel, while coal will be required to produce the synthetic liquid and gaseous fuels for those applications where solid fuels or electricity are not feasible. As the era of fossil fuels closes and the new age of atomic fusion and solar power is dawning, nuclear energy is absolutely essential. Without nuclear energy, we will not be able to develop and construct the fusion, solar, and other alternative sources required for the decades ahead.

Even though this section primarily focuses on nuclear energy, the underlying arguments are applicable to the entire energy security debate.

In the early days of nuclear power, the scare tactic was to allege that atomic power plants would become atomic bombs. After that nonsense was thoroughly discredited, the antinuclear movement charged that the radiation emitted by these power plants was deadly. This too was discredited, as was the subsequent scare campaign alleging that the cooling water discharges would boil our nation's rivers and lakes, destroying all fish and plant life.

Before 1977, the nation had been moving ahead with development of nuclear energy, despite the continuing propaganda efforts and guerrilla attacks. Then the antinuclear movement finally discovered a winning combination: 1) stop the breeder reactor program by using fabricated press releases concerning plutonium, 2) stop spent nuclear fuel reprocessing by making vague threats about terrorists who somehow are immune to radiation, 3) create serious doubts as to the future availability of spent fuel storage facilities, and 4) cripple the opportunities for our domestic nuclear industry to survive through exports by promoting the threat of nuclear weapon proliferation—while ignoring the reality that such prohibitions *actually increase* the threat of proliferation.

Each of these tactics has enjoyed success. But why do the opponents of nuclear energy continue to successfully advance even though the facts, data, evidence, and realities concerning nuclear energy discredit their positions? The answer, I believe, lies in Congress.

The opponents of nuclear energy have wrapped themselves in the invisible emperor's cloak of righteousness. They have assumed the role of good, while casting the proponents—who have surrendered the moral issues involved—as evil. The validity of this proposition can be demonstrated by talking with some of the men and women who support nuclear energy.

89

Even while disagreeing with the antinuclear crowd, nuclear power proponents still ascribe to their opponents pure and sincere motives. They are just "misguided idealists," trying to save mankind, even though they do not have all their facts straight. The supporters, on the other hand, are cast as being concerned only with such self-serving worries as jobs and profits.

It is time that the record be set straight. This battle for energy security cannot be won as long as the moral position is conceded to the opposition.

It is ironic that the moral defense offered for the American Nuclear Energy Program comes from a Russian. He is Andrei Sakharov, a Nobel Peace Prize winner in 1975 and prominent advocate of international disarmament, including the banning of nuclear weapons.

Doctor Sakharov has summarized perfectly the issue of nuclear energy. (His statement also provides a strong moral backing for the developers of other energy sources.) Dr. Sakharov states, "It is not just a question of comfort or maintaining what is called 'the quality of life.' It is a more important question—an issue of economic and political independence, of maintaining freedom for your children and your grandchildren."

That is the decision before us in the decade of the 1980s. Will the United States and its allies have the nuclear energy required for national independence and military defense, or will we continue our disastrous increasing dependence on outside energy sources?

Continued American dependence on Middle East oil does not benefit us nor the Arabs nor our other allies. It serves the best interest of only one nation—the Soviet Union. Reducing this dependence is essential if we are to maintain our ability to discourage Soviet aggression, not to mention preventing further decay of our dollar and our national economy.

The opponents of nuclear energy have one major advantage over the supporters. They are embarked on a quasi-religious crusade to rid mankind of the imagined horrors of the atom. Their position of self-perceived moral strength can easily override the factual arguments and logical presentations of energy security supporters, unless those of us who support energy growth understand that *our position* is morally correct. Those of us who support energy development must understand that *energy is a moral necessity* for mankind and that without it future generations will sink ever deeper into poverty and, eventually, dictatorship. Shortages of energy will result in shortages of jobs, housing, and food. And shortages of necessities—even when caused by government action—always result in increased government controls. Increased government controls will always lead to increased shortages. The tragic culmination of such a chain of events is war, as those who are without seek to take from those who have!

Dr. Sakharov understands very well the nature of the battle over nuclear energy. The question in Congress today is, "Do the supporters of energy security share Sakharov's understanding?" If we do not, but continue to concede the moral issue to our opponents, then it is only a matter of time before the Congress joins the Administration in performing the final rites over our nuclear energy program.

One American organization which also clearly understands the nature of the battle over energy is the NAACP. As the NAACP so accurately stated in a message of December, 1977, referring to President Carter's energy

91

plan, "We cannot accept the notion that our people are best served by a policy based upon the inevitability of energy shortages and the need for government to allocate an ever diminishing supply among competing interests."

The NAACP strongly believes that nuclear power *is vital* for the expansion of our economy, and that the problems posed by nuclear power "can be solved" through the dedicated efforts by government, the scientific community, and industry working cooperatively together.

It is important to examine the future energy demand situation, based on a projection of present policies.

Present trends can be misleading, however, as illustrated in the recent article "Why I Don't Believe in Energy Forecasts" written by Norman Macrae, deputy editor for *The Economist*. Mr. Macrae used a fictional forecaster, the Prophet of Munich, who was asked in 1928 to prophesy what life would be like in Germany in 5, 15, 20, and 40 years' time. He began by saying:

"My model prophesies that in five years' time, in 1933, Munich will be part of a Germany that has just had five million unemployed and that is newly ruled by an absolute dictator with a certifiable mental illness who will proceed to murder 10 million Jews, Gypsies and Slavs in the coldest of cold blood."

His audience said: "Oh dear, you must think then that in 15 years' time we will be in a sad plight."

"No," replied the Prophet, "my model says that in 1943 Munich will be part of a greater Germany whose flag will fly from Sebastopol to Bordeaux, from Norway's north cape to Tripoli, and that the standard of living of the German people in early 1943 will be 30 percent higher than that in any other European country except Sweden and the Vatican."

"Ach," said his audience, "you must then think that in 20 years' time we will be mighty indeed."

"No, my model says that in early 1948 Munich will be part of a Germany that is hemmed between the Elbe and the Rhine, and whose ruined heaps of cities will, at the end of 1947, have seen industrial production down at only 10 percent of the 1928 level."

Said his audience: "So you think we face black ruin in 40 years' time?"

"No, for 1968 my model prophesies that real income per head in Munich will be 350 percent higher than now in 1928, and that in the next year, 1969, 90 percent of German adults will sit looking at a box in a corner of their drawing rooms, which will show live color pictures of a man walking upon the Moon."

They locked him up as a loonie, of course.

This satirical analysis exposes the risk of forecasting. Nonetheless, forecasting our future energy needs is an important analytical tool in developing effective energy policy in the 1980s. We can project where our national energy demand is headed, using optimistic estimates for energy conservation impact, and then compare that to present energy supply. The result will give us the outlook for foreign oil imports. If energy conservation goals are not met, or domestic production does not achieve increased levels, then the import situation would be even worse.

We must look at a 20-year time period to develop our energy policy, because of the lead times required for introducing new technologies into the national energy system on a commercial scale. For example, about 25 years elapsed between the first successful demonstration of controlled nuclear fission and the operation of a commercial size nuclear power plant. And that was before the advent of the National Environmental Policy Act, the Clean Air Act, the Clean Water Act, and the host of other environmental and safety requirements imposed on new technologies. (I feel safe in saying that the automobile could not have been developed and mass-produced under present-day legislation; just as one illustration, imagine the response of the Congress and the regulatory agencies if an environmental impact statement for the automobile had been prepared projecting 50,000 traffic deaths a year). Assuming that energy conservation is effected nationwide and the economy recovers from its present slump, then a range of 2.5% to 3.5% for annual energy consumption growth would be a reasonable expectation for the period 1980-2000. An economy of reduced expectations, combined with effective energy conservation, might bring this down to the range of 1.5% to 2.5%.

For a 2.5% annual energy consumption growth rate, America would need approximately 64% additional energy supply by the year 2000, based on the supply available in 1980. If energy demand grows at 3.5% annually —a reasonable figure for a healthy, expanding economy using effective conservation measures—then nationwide America would need about a 100% increase in supply during that 20-year period. Even at the lower growth rate, between 1980 and 2000, America must add more than one new source of energy for every two existing in 1980. For example, this could mean building a new electric power plant for each two now built, or a new coal mine or new oil well for each two presently producing fuel.

In addition, as important as conservation is in America's overall energy effort, we must keep in mind that

94

conservation is not always energy efficient. In other words, there might be new energy demands where we would want to use a domestic energy source or conservation technique which would be less efficient than burning imported oil, due to national security and international economic considerations. While enabling us to meet our national needs, it would still require additional production of energy.

A further consideration is the necessity to decrease the present levels of American dependence on foreign oil, thereby requiring even more increases in domestic production. This realistic energy demand projection for 20 years illustrates the seriousness of our national energy dilemma. America must not only implement serious conservation policies and programs while simultaneously increasing domestic energy production to offset declines in present production sources and to meet increasing future energy demands, but must also address the critical problem of a dangerous dependency on foreign oil suppliers. Meeting this challenge will require a dramatic change in our nation's fundamental approach to energy policy decisions in the 1980s.

Recognizing the critical nature of our energy needs, America must develop a blueprint for domestic energy security: a balanced, reasoned, productive national energy program designed to eliminate our dependence on foreign oil imports and to ensure a reliable energy supply at the lowest possible cost.

The first issue to address is energy research and development. Many of the new technologies now being developed will not be commercialized until after the year 2000, but it is still essential that work on them be expedited now. It is not a question of solar versus nuclear, or wind versus coal, or shale oil versus synthetic gas from coal. *All* of these technologies will be needed, together with geothermal energy, alcohol fuels from agricultural products, electric vehicles, and electricity from waste products.

However, it is essential to remember that, for the next two decades, America will still depend primarily on oil, natural gas, coal, nuclear energy, and hydroelectric power for our energy needs. *The next generation will use what this generation develops.* The Carter Administration's projections for synthetic fuels production are overly optimistic, but even they point up the relatively small amounts of synthetic fuels that can be made available for use before the end of this century. Large-scale commercialization of atomic fusion and solar energy, and as-yet-unknown scientific breakthroughs will occur in the 21st century. For the next twenty years, we are limited to the technologies *presently* known to us. And in order to ensure the quality of life which our political system is capable of achieving during the next twenty years and the decades to follow, we must develop them all.

To realize this goal, America must recognize that the primary obstacles to such development are *not* scientific and engineering problems, nor financial and business problems, but are the legislative and regulatory roadblocks imposed by the Congress and the Administration.

The basic step in moving ahead with a balanced, productive energy program is to *reexamine existing environmental controls,* especially the Clean Air Act, the Clean Water Act, and federal land use policies and regulations. In the 1980s we must revise the myriad of provisions which have no beneficial impact on human health and well-being. Congress can "fine tune" those controls which must be maintained, but which involve serious procedural problems. And Congress must reevaluate those goals which may be unnecessarily strict. I am confident that our technology can provide the environmental protection necessary, while meeting the nation's energy needs.

The next requirement for domestic energy security is a *total overhaul* of existing government policies and controls that adversely affect our goal of decreasing foreign oil imports. The most glaring example of such counterproductive measures is the Energy Policy and Conservation Act of 1975 (EPCA).

I believe that it is essential that the facts about this act be understood and exposed. The counterproductive energy policy legislation being pushed through in Congress by some of my liberal colleagues is basically an extension of the philosophy and policies of the EPCA. If the public learns that our present-day dangerous and growing dependence on OPEC oil is a result of the EPCA and that the extension of its philosophy will increase our dependency, then we stand a better chance to develop rational energy policy alternatives in the 1980s.

There were two key policy decisions made in 1975. The first related directly to oil imports. Basically, Congress decided to extend and formalize the so-called entitlements program. To those not familiar with this strange policy, it requires that Americans who refine predominantly American-produced crude oil must pay a subsidy to those Americans who refine predominantly foreign-produced crude oil. Its stated purpose was to equalize the burdens of price control, but it predictably discouraged domestic oil production and increased foreign oil imports.

The second mistaken energy policy that resulted from the energy conference of 1975 was the so-called composite price structure. This was a vehicle to continue the price controls imposed on American oil. The price controls have been continued, according to a formula which guaranteed that any percentage increase in new oil production would automatically require a decrease in the ceiling price for all new oil.

This inconsistency with the stated purpose of the Energy Policy and Conservation Act of 1975 was just as obvious then as it is now. In fact, several of us on the conference (which is a meeting of Senate and House members to resolve differences) pointed out the mathematical certainty that the composite price structure would *increase* oil imports. The composite price structure mandated by law that increases in the production of new oil in the United States would require decreases in the ceiling price allowed for new oil.

The results of the EPCA were predictable. Government energy reports are sad evidence of the inevitable outcome of a politically-spawned, irrational attempt to continue the energy philosophies typified by natural gas price controls. In 1973, total direct oil imports from OPEC were slightly under three million barrels per day. For the first seven months of 1977, America imported *over six* million barrels per day directly from OPEC. Even more significant are the figures for the Arab members of OPEC. In 1973, America imported less than one million barrels per day. For the first seven months of 1977, our imports from the Arab members of OPEC exceeded three million barrels per day. And this was *after* the Arab Oil Embargo in 1973 and the passage of the Energy Policy and Conservation Act of 1975. (Who says Congress just talks and talks, but can never accomplish anything? Here we have a situation where the Arabs embargo oil exports and the Congress manages to pass *a law which triples Arab oil imports* in less than four years!)

As I sat in the Senate during Congressional deliberations on EPCA, I was amazed at how the supporters of the EPCA managed to gain support from the Federal Energy Administration and the oil industry for this counterproductive legislation. Their main argument was that "the controls are only temporary." Under the EPCA, price controls on oil were to end after 39 months.

At the time, there were many of us who knew that this deadline was illusory. The 39-month figure was just a face-saver for those who knew the EPCA was a bad law, but who also believed that politics required approval. The Carter Administration has now decided that the controls will be partially removed, but only if a so-called windfall profits tax is imposed. As those who have studied this proposal know, the tax really has nothing to do with profits, but is an excise tax which will provide the federal government with windfall revenues, and will be paid by the American consumer. In addition, the basic approach of the Administration scheme is an extension of the EPCA. In the short run, some politicians will make political gains, but in the long run domestic production will be less, foreign oil imports will be higher, and the nation will suffer.

The results will speak for themselves and many of those responsible for the EPCA are still urging a continuation into the 1980s of the disastrous energy policy upon which the EPCA is based. What is necessary is to send a loud, clear message to Congress that the American public *will not* be fooled again. The time has come to tell the Congress that no longer can public officials avoid doing what has to be done, just to avoid political criticism. In 1973, there may have been some excuse for ignorance about the energy issue and its significance for our society, even though the crisis warnings had been sounded—and substantiated—for years. The Arab Oil Embargo of 1973-74 was not the first—nor last. In 1957, 1967, and 1970, there were supply interruptions from Arab oil fields. But, during those cutoffs, the United States had excess productive capacity, so that we could meet our own needs and even help out our allies. But that ended in 1971. As a result the cutoffs of 1973-74 and 1979 produced a shock wave which dramatically showed that *energy is the lifeblood* of a modern civilization. The thought of 200 million people fighting for scarce supplies of energy should cause even the most ardent antienergy person to pause and reconsider.

Our energy debate today is being carefully watched by people, both here and overseas, who will be making decisions such as:

"Are United States dollar-based securities really secure?"

"Will the United States demand that foreign oil production be pushed even higher than present levels?"

And most important, "Does the United States Government have the courage and integrity to ignore the demands of antienergy, antiindustrial opponents, of progress, or will its national energy policy continue in the 1980s to be based on disproven tenets which allow politicians to support policies that *create* the exact crisis which they supposedly are trying to prevent?

With over four billion people in the world today, increased energy is absolutely vital to ensure that peace and well-being are maintained and extended. As just one example, food production alone will demand an ever-increasing share of fossil fuel energy and its derivatives. We must work now to avoid future debates over whether fossil fuels should be used for fertilizers and agricultural needs or for transportation and industrial needs.

In the 1980s, our energy blueprint should include:

1. Continued research and development of advanced energy sources, emphasizing electricity from solar energy and fusion energy, with the earliest possible commercialization. Americans should hope for technological breakthroughs during the next two decades, but realize that large-scale facilities will not be available before the year 2000.

2. Continued research and development of synthetic fuels from coal and shale, with commercialization during the last decade. Substantial quantities of fuel should become available in the first decade of the 21st century.

3. Continued research and development, with rapidly increasing commercialization, of alternative technologies which can begin to meet specific energy needs now. Among these technologies are solar heating and cooling, alcohol fuels from agricultural products and waste materials, geothermal energy for both electricity generation and process heat, electric vehicles for urban transportation use, and wind devices producing electricity. These technologies and others, such as hydrogen-fueled systems, are already being used on an individual basis or in unique circumstances. As experience grows and performance improves, their use will become more widespread.

4. Continued construction of electric power plants using coal and nuclear fuel, with increasing emphasis on breeder reactors using reprocessed fuel from existing light water reactors.

5. Utilization of available hydroelectric resources,

with emphasis on smaller projects requiring less capital investment.

6. Increased production of domestic coal, oil, and natural gas, including undeveloped areas such as offshore regions.

The realization of these six points will require that Congress limit the federal government's role in energy security to the *creation of the political and economic climate* necessary for progress. The government is not qualified to decide which technology should be developed or commercialized. Our present energy dilemma is the result primarily of government mistakes and political posturings. We can reverse that policy.

I am confident that once the American people have the facts surrounding our present energy dilemma and how we got here, they will demand the implementation of an energy program based on production and conservation, not government regulation and decreases in the standard of living.

HEALTH CARE
MAKING A GOOD SYSTEM BETTER

By SENATOR RICHARD S. SCHWEIKER

Health care in America today suffers from indulgence. The symptoms are a plethora of financing, calories, and self-deceiving lifestyles. Pointing a finger of blame serves little purpose.

It is time to change course, to preserve the best of the past, and to embark on a broad-scale initiative to make Americans *more aware* of viable health options.

I am convinced that when Americans understand the need to change their diets, their lifestyles, and the health care delivery system, they will respond positively.

In the short term, we need to reset financial incentives in the health care delivery structure to raise the cost consciousness of the professionals, the patients, and the institutions.

Resetting those incentives simply involves increasing good, old-fashioned *competition* within the system of hospitals, clinics, medical groups, the health insurers, and—to the extent possible—by the patients themselves.

Arguments abound in government and within the industry about how much health care is needed. The quantitative answer is that no one knows. Other subjective measurements must be made in terms of quality, availability, and incidence of major illness.

There is no argument, however, that pluralistic delivery modes provide both a choice and financial alternatives. The best known of these is the health maintenance organization (HMO)—which offers a wide array of health services for a fixed monthly fee.

This contrasts with the traditional fee-for-service offered by physicians in an individual office setting. There are all sorts of variations between.

HMOs hold the promise of dramatic savings, primarily by reducing hospitalization, but as yet care for less than 5% of the nation.

The federal government—which has seen the cost of health care rise from 5.9% of the gross national product in 1965 to 8.8% in 1977 and which, in fiscal 1980, expects to spend $55-60 billion for health-related services —believes it has a stake in change.

The government is a major purchaser of health care, and has a legitimate role in ensuring the health and safety of its citizens. Because of this, as ranking Republican on the Senate Labor and Human Resources Committee and the Senate Appropriations Labor-HEW Appropriations Subcommittee, I have been an active participant in the development of health policy.

In this chapter I will attempt to define some of the issues (comprehensive health reform, health manpower, food and drugs, biomedical research, nutrition) and to propose some solutions which may be appropriate for the next decade.

COMPREHENSIVE HEALTH REFORM

As the single largest purchaser of health services, the government now accounts for over 40 percent of all health spending in America. Medicare and Medicaid alone paid $43 billion in 1978 for health costs of their beneficiaries. The increasing health care payments by the federal government are exceeded only by its intrusions into the affairs of health care institutions. We can all agree the government has a responsibility to spend tax money properly. But that does not give it the right to tell health care managers how to run their institutions. The costs of this intrusion have become painfully clear.

The government has imposed administrative requirements and red tape burdens which often lead to the strangulation of the *very industry we are trying to help*. Among health care delivery organizations in particular, these burdens have had a demonstrable effect on efficiency and competition. I asked the Washington Health Center, a District of Columbia hospital, to furnish me with regulations it must comply with at the district and federal levels.

Federal regulations alone overflowed a four-wheeled metal shopping market basket. Local regulations filled another. I was delighted to display the crammed federal basket for national television during a Health Subcommittee hearing on hospital cost containment. Government regulation has cast a confusing and irritating shadow over all of us.

In health care, we have reached the crossroads. Some of us in Congress have heeded the signs CAUTION, DANGER AHEAD, and are responding to the health care industry and to the American public. We are choosing, not further regulation, but to pursue free market competition.

Let me take a moment to explain how we got to this point in American health policy in the first place and some lessons we have learned. For at least thirty years the health care policy of this nation has pursued the goal that, in health care, more is better.

Through the 1950s, 60s, and 70s, more and more government money has been spent—

105

—to construct more hospitals;

—to train more physicians, nurses, dentists, and other professionals;

—to provide more services to the elderly, the poor, migrants, Indians, and other groups;

—to construct more research facilities;

—and to generate ever more sophisticated health care technology.

Three decades ago a large part of this country did not have access to good health care. And, to be sure, these programs *were* milestones for the people they helped.

In some ways, though, these programs were too successful. Many places in the country now have too many doctors, too many hospitals, and too much expensive equipment. All these health services have to be paid for —through higher insurance premiums, and through increased medical costs.

In health care, we've reached the point where more is *no longer* better. The watchwords now are "restraint" and "efficiency." We've got an inflationary spiral on our hands that has to be stopped. Otherwise health care will be out of reach for the average citizen.

The Carter Administration's answer to the health care dilemma is still the same old litany—more government regulation. In Congress we've spent more than two years wading through the complexities of the Administration's regulatory hospital cost containment plan—"inpatient revenue increase limits," "wage pass-throughs," and "volume load adjustments." All it has done is make us wonder how in the world the U.S. Congress could get so tangled up in the hospital administration business.

Martin Feldstein, a noted Harvard health economist, testified before the Senate Health Subcommittee that the Administration's cost control bill would limit the quantity and quality of hospital care. Yet the measure would have little economic impact. For instance, by 1984, the measure would save less than $150 for a family of four with a $30,000 annual income. Moreover, the accumulated impact on inflation is almost unnoticeable; only four-tenths of one percent over five years (assuming a 6 percent annual inflation rate). This economist suggested that the same economic savings could be achieved without regulations by increasing the average coinsurance rate from 10 percent to 14 percent.

Until an issue like cost containment came along, the consequences of the regulatory approach were not clear. After all, some regulation of health care is generally accepted as necessary to protect the public's health and welfare. But with this growing acceptance, we moved from health and safety regulations to economic regulation. Legislation has brought restriction by the government on market opportunities, investment decisions, and even pricing. This is not only new to the health care industry, but it is a fateful step away from free-market competition and private sector control. It's a step toward what Ralph Nader calls "Uncle Sam, the Monopoly Man."

The time Congress has spent on cost containment has taught us one critical lesson—and this is one of the key points I wish to make—that it is imperative that the health care industry succeed in reducing costs, improving access, and maintaining quality *on its own.*

Private sector initiatives deserve greater credit in Washington than they are getting. For instance, the "voluntary effort" initiated by hospital and other health care leaders has demonstrated that private sector alternatives *can* work, if given the chance.

Despite double digit inflation, the medical care component of the consumer price index rose less than the index itself during each of the first eight months of this year. And even though inflation in the general economy has accelerated, increases in hospital expenses for the first half of 1979 remained virtually the same as during the first half of 1978 when the voluntary effort achieved its goal. (We can only wish that the food and oil industries could match that performance.)

On another front, our nation's major employers—private corporations—have launched a campaign of their own to stabilize costs for health benefits to their employes. Working individually or together in groups, businesses have put the health care field on notice that they intend to actively seek solutions to excessive health costs.

In July 1979, I wrote to several hundred of the country's largest corporations, sharing my views on national health care reform and soliciting their opinions.

The responses I received revealed a variety of successful and encouraging initiatives to address rising health care costs. For instance:

—greater use of utilization review committees to monitor hospital care paid by all third parties;
—greater cost sharing by employes;
—incentives for increased and less costly delivery of health services such as outpatient care, ambulatory surgery, home health care, and disease prevention activities;
—insurance coverage for second and even third opinions on elective surgery;
—intramural programs stressing health promotion and health education.

Corporations have become laboratories for creative solutions to combat the trend toward high cost coverage. A few larger firms such as Scott Paper Company, R. J. Reynolds Industries, Uniroyal Inc., and Ford Motor Company have developed health maintenance organizations as one option for their employes. In order to put the lid on their escalating premium costs, many businesses are negotiating with their insurers for cost saving features such as pre-admission testing and utilization review, second opinion surgery programs, and cost sharing for certain services.

Nonconventional approaches now being embraced by some companies are aimed at health promotion and health education. Clinics on smoking, alcoholism, and mental stress, physical fitness programs, nutrition and diet counseling are just a few of the activities being offered to employes. While these efforts have high start-up costs and no offsetting tax breaks, employers are attracted to the promise of more productive, satisfied workers with lower rates of absenteeism. These truly private sector initiatives *should be cultivated* in an environment free from government interference.

The stake these companies have in containing costs will no doubt spur them to greater involvement. The pressure these employers exert on providers will eventually spread through the entire health care system to the benefit of all.

The country's major insurers also deserve credit for cooperating in these cost saving ventures and for initiating many of their own. Their willingness to foster and support a variety of health care delivery models and reimbursement innovations has created more competition among providers. These efforts must be nurtured and allowed to bloom—*without* government interference.

In this new political climate, brought about partly as a backlash to the Administration's cost containment debacle, the quest by some for national health insurance—federally controlled—begins anew.

National health insurance is believed to be by some the great unfinished project of the great society, the ultimate vision of the days when more was better. Its controlling principle is that the best way to give all Americans good health care is with more health insurance—courtesy of the federal government.

I call this way of thinking—the National Health Insurance Dream. And the legislative proposals supporting this dream are a nightmare!

I say this because, if we've learned anything, it's that using government programs to solve social problems *does not work* very well.

The following example of good intentions gone awry came to my attention late in 1979:

The law requires that big and small employers give women the opportunity to fill jobs traditionally held—and rightfully so—by men. A Philadelphia construction contractor found that he could not hire two-tenths of one female, even though the bureaucrats make him wish he had. He had no office, no secretary, and only three employes. He also had a federal contract and four laborer jobs that came under affirmative action—but no women. And because an Executive Order requires a so-called goal of 5% female laborers, the U.S. Labor Department stepped in, demanding that he agree to a number of requirements or be prohibited from bidding on any future federal jobs.

The contractor didn't like it, but he agreed. The requirements, which covered 10 pages and listed 43 records to be kept and actions to be taken, included: designating an equal employment opportunity officer; posting EEO notices; writing to minority and women's groups announcing apprenticeship programs; posting notices of parties and picnics; and providing separate rest room facilities.

This is a *total waste* of government resources and a small businessman's time. I have asked the Labor Secretary to take immediate corrective action by exempting employers with less than 25 workers from these affirmative action rules.

We have learned that more health insurance can likewise be part of the problem, not the cure. Ninety percent of all Americans now have some form of public or private health insurance. More than 90 percent of all hospital bills are paid not directly by the patient, but by insurance companies or the government. So much health care insurance is available that no one—not patients, not doctors, not hospitals—has any incentive to hold down costs. Health insurance gives everyone an unlimited expense account. (In turn, health cost prices have gotten so high that *bankruptcy resulting from catastrophic illness expenses* has become a major national concern.)

President Carter's chief inflation fighter, Alfred Kahn, summed up the problem perfectly on ABC-TV's Good Morning America in late 1979. He said, "We've got a crazy system for delivering health in which the patient doesn't pay; 90 to 95% of the hospital bills are paid by third parties. They're not paid by the consumer who pays the premiums to the insurance company, and they're not paid by the doctor who decides how much will be provided. There's no accountability. There's no incentive."

The recent experience of two countries with national health programs provides further evidence against an expanding government role in health care. In Great Britain, forty thousand electrical workers from one of Britain's most powerful unions elected to subscribe to the *private* health care system. Their defection is a clear indication of dissatisfaction with the state-run system of medical care. For example, waiting a year for elective surgery is common. Patients for hip replacements and tonsillectomies must wait 2-3 years. Several other unions and the 5.3 million-member automobile association are considering a similar move. Though still less than 5% of total health care outlays in Great Britain the private health sector has doubled since 1975.

Last year, in an unprecedented move, Australia voted to "reprivatize" its once highly acclaimed medibank system of national health care. Fear of higher government taxes to pay for continually rising costs under this system (which increased 20 percent in 1977 compared to general inflation of 14 percent) prompted the pullout. A government spokesman admitted, "This change is a victory for the private nonprofit health-insurance funds. Health insurance will no longer be compulsory. People will have a choice of private insurance or accepting government benefits." The Australians found it necessary to restore balance to their health care system in order to contain costs. The message to this nation in both these experiences is obvious.

In the face of this evidence, the Administration's health bill, S. 1912, Senator Kennedy's plan, S. 1720, and even the catastrophic approach proposed by Senators Long and Ribicoff, S. 350 and S. 351, rely on centralized government regulation and increased federal expenditures as the "solution." In fact, they would just prolong the nightmare.

Our health system is ailing. What it needs is a stiff dose of competition. On July 26, I introduced in the Senate a comprehensive health care reform bill that encourages incentives *within the existing system* to control costs, and targets health insurance coverage to the areas of greatest need.

There are other health policymakers seeking health

112

care reform using an approach similar to the one in my bill—whose cosponsors are Republican Senators Schmitt of New Mexico, Laxalt of Nevada, Hatch of Utah, Cohen of Maine, Thurmond of South Carolina, and Bellmon of Oklahoma.

For example, Senator Durenberger (R-Minn.), and Congressman James Jones (R-Ok.) have introduced tax-related proposals with multiple health plan requirements for employers. Congressman Al Ullman (D-Oreg.), Chairman of the House Ways and Means Committee, incorporates a copayment feature designed to induce cost containment. What these legislative proposals all have in common with my plan is *restructuring incentives using the tax system to promote consumer choice and competition* among insurers and providers. They all attempt to halt the trend toward fixed dollar, comprehensive health insurance coverage. They either do this through requiring copayment on certain services, as contained in my bill, or by placing a ceiling on tax deductible health insurance premiums of employers, or both. They all recognize that the average American family needs financial protection from medical catastrophe and have provided limits on out-of-pocket medical expenses during the year.

My plan is the private sector alternative to national health insurance. It contains four main elements:

First: It encourages employers, through tax incentives, to offer employes a choice of three separate health care plans. The employer's dollar contribution to each plan is required to be the same. This choice promotes competition among health insurers, encouraging lower premiums and better benefits for employes.

Second: At least one of these plans must include a 25 percent cost sharing—or copayment—provision for hospital services. Several noted health economists have testified that involving patients in hospital care decisions will inevitably reduce hospital costs. That will challenge providers to be more efficient. As an added incentive, employes choosing the low-cost option will receive a tax-free rebate for the premium difference.

These two provisions alone would save $10 billion annually to the health care system by 1983.

Third: My catastrophic provision protects an individual or family once the out-of-pocket costs reach 20 percent of family wages. I believe this catastrophic trigger based on family income from wages is a more equitable approach than a fixed dollar level. All employers with 50 or more employees would be required to provide this catastrophic protection. A pooling arrangement by private insurers and states will allow access for small-firm employes, uninsurable risks, and others seeking insurance to catastrophic health coverage. Additionally, my bill expands Medicare by providing older people better protection against catastrophic illness. Currently, Medicare limits such coverage. Further, it would insure that no one in this country would need to face the threat and fear of medical bankruptcy.

Fourth: As a condition for tax deduction, my proposal encourages all employers to offer a preventive health benefits package comprised of such preventive measures as pre- and postnatal care for mothers and infants, childhood immunizations, hypertension screening, cervical cancer, and periodic health examinations. I am also considering incentives to employers who initiate health education and health promotion programs for their employes. These programs might include exercise, diet or weight control, nonsmoking classes, or alcoholism clinics. Americans are increasingly interested in taking positive measures to stay healthy and remain well. Moreover, studies show that business can gain as much as employes. Health promotion lowers absenteeism, improves morale, and productivity. I feel it is time we stopped paying lip service to health promotion—disease prevention activities—and used them to reduce health costs. I suspect that we spend more money in this country for get-well cards than we do for health prevention!

These four features I believe, appropriately address the issues of cost containment, catastrophic illness, and disease prevention in a comprehensive and consistent manner. They do so, not through further regulation, or by setting up costly new government programs. It can be done by rearranging federal tax incentives to *attack the root cause* of all three problems. The root cause is the third party reimbursement buffer. It is subsidized by federal tax deductions for health insurance premiums. It is noncompetitive. And, it is heavily slanted toward fixed-dollar insurance coverage that is used most often for short term hospital care.

Another area which offers great promise for containing costs as well as stimulating competition among health providers is the prepaid health plan of "health maintenance organization."

Congress singled out this approach toward health care delivery for special attention in several pieces of legislation in the late '70s. HMO's have received favorable treatment for their impressive record in reducing hospital utilization and emphasis on health maintenance.

Passage of the HMO amendments of 1978, which I authored, repaired many of the shortcomings in the HMO law. The revised health planning law of 1979 put HMOs on an equal footing with physician offices concerning certification-of-need authority. The perception of HMOs as potential competition in the health delivery environment earned them a reprieve from the planning process. Proof of congressional support for this concept was a doubling of the appropriation for the federal HMO program in fiscal 1980.

Some health policymakers believe the cost saving features of prepaid health plans should serve as the "model" for national health financing policy. However, I firmly support the notion that a variety of health delivery models be developed and promoted. We should not devote all our resources to one approach. There ought to be *many* incentives in the health care marketplace which encourage physicians and institutional providers to look for innovative practice arrangements.

My bill introduces incentives into the existing system to involve the consumers of health care more actively and directly into hospital service pricing decisions. Employers will force insurers to be more competitive. The insurers, in turn, will prod the providers to greater efficiency. The result, under my proposal, would be an estimated net saving of $3.7 billion annually to the health care system.

The hospital cost containment debate has provided a unique opportunity to respond to the demands for greater access and better quality at a reasonable cost. How far we get with health care reform is everyone's responsibility. And across the country, coalitions of business, labor, insurance, health care, and civic leaders are responding in geographic areas. One such group is the Philadelphia Area Committee on Health Care Costs, formed in 1977. The 70-member committee created a number of task forces looking into various health care delivery problems, including overbedding, maldistribution of health professionals and energy conservation.

The energy task force provided $1.5 million in private funds for an evaluation and installation of energy-saving devices at certain health facilities. In 18 months, that effort has resulted in about $5 million in energy savings for those institutions.

For thousands of others, in communities where local Health Systems Agencies are established, the 1974 Health Planning law provides a formal opportunity to help agencies shape their health care delivery systems. This approach requires strong public participation. The country must choose between a government-controlled health system and one which emphasizes the competitive private sector. The choices are clear.

HEALTH MANPOWER

The Health Professions Educational Assistance Act is an excellent example of high impact legislation that has helped alter circumstances. Its primary purpose has been the expansion and improvement of institutions to train physicians, dentists, and other health professionals.

The history of this legislation, beginning in 1963, reflects a federal commitment to assure that the right number and type of professionals will be available to serve our health needs. We knew in 1963 that we had a shortage of doctors, but we didn't know how many more physicians we needed or whether we could significantly improve the situation through legislation.

Yet the situation was acute. It was clear that the private sector could not respond alone. Congress started by providing a loan program for health professions students and a construction grant program for their schools.

117

As the decade progressed and the magnitude of the problem became clearer (in 1969 it was estimated that the U.S. had a shortage of at least 50,000 doctors), the Congress became more active, eventually providing institutional support grants to schools willing to expand enrollments. By all appearances, this effort means there will not be a shortage of doctors within 5 to 10 years. The number of medical students has more than doubled—from 32,000 in the early 1960s to 65,000 today. This was accomplished by incentives, not mandates. Some, including the new Department of Health and Human Services (formerly DHEW), even predict that there will soon be too many doctors. But a potential surplus of physicians is one of the essential elements of my optimism for the 1980s and beyond.

Why? The expanding number of physicians means competition.

Because of the long pipeline (7-10 years) between enrollment in medical school and the completion of residency training, we have not yet seen the full impact that increased numbers of physicians will have on our health care system. However, there are already some visible signs, mostly hopeful, that competition in the delivery of health care services is real. For example, there is an increasing willingness of young doctors to settle in rural areas, presumably because there is a demand for their services and considerably less competition during the financially shaky early years of setting up a practice. We will soon see also a far more satisfactory balance between primary care providers and specialists. The Health Manpower Act exemplifies the very best type of federal problem-solving: meet the interim needs and focus on ways to help the private sector solve the long-run problems.

During the 1960s and 1970s, the health care "expectations" of the American people created a demand that could not be met. Meanwhile the doctors needed to meet this demand were still in training. As a consequence government became deeply involved in running programs to provide health care services directly to communities.

These programs—community health centers, migrant health programs, Indian health services, the National Health Service Corps, emergency medical services—have served a valuable purpose in meeting vital interim needs. As we enter the 1980s each must be reevaluated to see if the needs still exist. If so, we must encourage the private sector or state and local governments to do the job.

SAFE FOOD AND DRUGS

Advances in medical and drug technology and infinite variations in foodstuffs over the years have layered regulations over their production. Like the initial support of the health care delivery system, federal protection began as a boon and is now the bane of the public and the producers.

Among the most widely accepted federal regulatory functions are those to ensure the safety of foods and the safety and effectiveness of drugs and medical devices. Since the passage of the Pure Food and Drug Act of 1906, Americans have looked to the Food and Drug Administration to protect them from dangerous substances in foods and from risky or fraudulently-promoted medicines.

Yet over the years, our evolving scientific technology and increasingly sophisticated ability to detect risks, compounded by long years of bureaucratic expansionism, have led to major problems of over-regulation. Increasing regulatory burdens have serious economic repercussions as well, even though the basic purpose remains related to consumer health and safety.

Regulatory compliance costs frequently depress competition and innovation by driving out small businesses and making private industry less willing to invest in new ideas and new products.

The consumer bears the ultimate burden of excessive regulation in higher costs for the goods he buys and decreased opportunity for choices in the marketplace.

Food safety is a clear example of a field in which scientific sophistication *has outstripped* the provisions of current law administered by the FDA. The Delaney clause of the Federal Food, Drug and Cosmetic Act flatly requires a ban on any food additive shown by appropriate scientific tests to induce cancer in man or animal, regardless of any benefit it might offer.

This provision served us well for two decades. Its purpose—to ensure that unsafe, cancer-causing substances do not enter the food supply—remains valid. Today, however, we can detect substances in foods at levels of parts per billion, technically far more minute than we could detect in 1960. We can identify extremely weak carcinogens. Even if food contains only a minute quantity of a substance which—when fed in extremely high doses to test animals—produces a weak cancer-causing effect, its use as a food additive must be banned. It does not matter if the substance offers health benefits which might outweigh a small risk of cancer. The law does not provide for that consideration.

Clearly, we cannot have a risk-free food supply. As the notorious saccharin case so vividly illustrates, the public neither expects nor desires such an unrealistic policy. The answer, embodied in food additive safety legislation I introduced, is to provide for risk-benefit assessment.

Such assessments cannot be precise, because science is unable to quantify risks or set forth a safe "no effect" threshold level for carcinogens. FDA officials have argued against changing the law for this reason. (For once, they do not seem to want discretionary authority.)

Undeniably, the risk-benefit approach will complicate the regulator's life and make his job more difficult. But it cannot be avoided if we are to have a realistic food safety policy that is responsive to the consumer's legitimate needs.

Public outcry in the saccharin case also pointed up Americans' desire to place limits on the decisions government makes for us "for our own good." Even when the risk-benefit assessment may militate against allowing unrestricted use of an additive in bulk foods for most people, it may offer advantages to other consumers. Informed individual choice should come into play. Consumers should be given the facts—in some cases, a warning label on the product may even be called for—but individuals *should* have the opportunity to make a rational choice.

One major piece of new health regulatory legislation considered (by the Senate) in the 96th Congress involved the controls on prescription and over-the-counter drugs. Regulation of the development, approval, marketing, promotion, and use of drugs in the United States has grown increasingly complex and burdensome since 1906. Regulatory overkill results have been predictable: excessive paperwork, increasingly long delays in the approval of new drugs, more and more detailed manufacturing and packaging requirement, and unrealistic limitations on drug exports which hurt American companies and unfairly penalized American workers. Some of us in Congress have long recognized that our drug laws *actually depress* incentives for needed new drugs and exporting American research, technology, and jobs overseas.

During the 95th Congress, the Administration presented "regulatory reform" proposals—a skeptical designation, I have learned. The actual effect is a regulatory morass.

A Republican perspective sets the goals of any true "reform" legislation at eliminating unnecessary regulation and improving the performance and accountability of regulatory agencies.

Particularly in drug regulatory reform, key goals should encourage innovative research to develop and make available safe and effective therapies for American consumers, to improve medical practice drug therapies.

Significant advances in the area of diabetes, for example, came out in testimony before my committees. That disease is one of the nation's leading causes of blindness. But laser beam technology combined with other new treatment has meant that people who were legally blind now can see. Those who used to face the near-certain prospect of blindness now have hope.

DNA (the chemical letters describing the basic human cell) technology is holding out the promise of synthesizing human insulin for diabetes victims.

These goals and results led me to introduce my own drug bill (S. 1138) and to press for a substantial rewrite of legislation before the Health Subcommittee. Measures that begin to "deregulate" the earliest phases of drug research and allow drug developers to bypass FDA at this stage were included. Procedures were mandated to expedite resolution of legitimate scientific disputes between regulators and drug sponsors and allow research to proceed without undue delay.

Administration proposals to give the FDA sweeping new civil penalty authority and allow the FDA to take companies directly to court, bypassing the Justice Department, were eliminated. Republicans also supported liberalizing our drug export policy, which cripples U.S. manufacturers' foreign market sales by prohibiting drugs not approved for use in the United States, and to guard against the proliferation of new burdensome and conflicting regulations.

The primacy of private sector drug research, threatened by proposals to establish a federal center for new drug studies, was strengthened by my clarifying amendments that government research may be implemented only if the private sector is not planning or conducting similar research.

Most importantly, emphasis was placed on the need to speed up FDA procedures so that drugs will reach the consumer sooner. In addition, companies must have the assurance that valuable trade secrets submitted to the FDA will be protected. My amendments specifically prohibit disclosure of trade secrets.

A final point in drug regulation reform involves the approval of so-called generic equivalents of drugs marketed since 1962. FDA has interpreted current law to require subsequent manufacturers of previously approved drugs to demonstrate all over again that the drug is safe and effective.

Compelling "second" manufacturers to reinvent the wheel entails high costs (in some cases, more than $10 million in tests) and inhibits competition. It also may be ethically questionable to subject humans to drug studies when a safe and effective treatment for their illness already is available.

My drug bill and my amendments to the Health Committee drug legislation addressed this issue squarely. They establish an abbreviated "true equivalency" approval procedure for subsequent manufacturers of approved drugs on the market for at least seven years. This limited testing would cost only about $30,000 per drug. Companies will continue to have full patent protection for innovative products.

In all industries some can be expected to resent opening the market to more competition. Large firms can better afford the compliance costs of regulations which shield them from some competitive pressures. Barriers to market entry to newcomers—such as a requirement that competitors shoulder as much as $10 million in testing costs—are clearly desired by the firm that gets on the market first, since costs tend to ensure something close to monopoly market position. But *many firms* should be able to do the limited drug equivalence testing. American consumers and the competitive sector benefit.

BIOMEDICAL RESEARCH

Health research is an investment in better health and quality of life for all Americans. The federal government today supports the majority of all biomedical and behavioral research in the United States, through the National Institutes of Health (NIH) and the National Science Foundation (NSF).

Our government research support represents a rather unique partnership between the public and private sectors.

In some countries, government bureaucrats decide

what research should be done and which ideas pursued. In the United States, most federally-supported health research is done through privately-initiated grants. Proposals generated by outstanding researchers outside of government are reviewed for scientific and technical merit by scientific peer groups. The mutually beneficial blending of public and private sectors helps ensure the flow of fresh, innovative research ideas. It has resulted in a biomedical research capacity of unparalleled excellence, one of our great national resources.

But sometimes federal health research misses the mark. In 1971, some of my constituents pointed out to me that diabetes, for which there is no known cure, was being "neglected." No one at the National Institutes of Health had a primary responsibility for it. Also, diabetes research was underfunded. Per capita research was about $4 compared to $700 per patient with cancer.

Under my 1974 legislation, a fact-finding diabetes commission recommended a five-year funding plan for NIH research and a state control program under the Center for Disease Control.

My 1976 legislation put this plan in action, and today diabetes draws a fairer share of disease research funding.

Basic research funding is an appropriate federal role. In most cases, the payoff is not clear immediately, and the private sector is not willing or able to make the substantial investment required. As our knowledge expands and strengthens in a given field, much applied research and development is taken over by the private sector. An example is DNA technology. NIH-sponsored researchers have done basic studies on understanding the cell and ways to combine genetic material from different cells. The federal role should only underwrite basic research and fill in the gaps left by the private sector while the *private sector* should have primary interest and responsibility for the development and application of the basic findings.

As budgets shrink, it becomes more important to encourage private industry to invest in innovative research and development.

Government patent policies and tax incentives should be reevaluated to promote the public-private research continuum, particularly in areas which may have little commercial value, such as the development of new treatments for relatively rare diseases.

NUTRITION

By and large, the main issues addressed so far in this chapter have dealt with the payment for curative health. But the profoundest impact on reducing those costs rests with a generational campaign to induce people to choose to be healthy in the first place. We have a long way to go.

It is hard to ignore the importance of nutrition to health. The body's nutritional requirements are influenced not only by diet, but by exercise, tobacco, alcohol, and stress. And these factors—which respect neither class nor status—contribute to much of the illness that afflicts Americans today. The greatest challenge we face is keeping our people healthy.

Unfortunately, medical education and research have concentrated on *medical cure* rather than health care.

As an example of the inadequacies inherent in a fragmented, disease-oriented approach to health care, a young doctor told me of the story of how the highly sophisticated, organized, medical care system failed an elderly patient in Philadelphia:

126

The woman had been hospitalized for an acute illness. However, the doctors reached the sad conclusion that, although her acute disorder had been satisfactorily treated, the woman was "irreversibly senile." She did not know where she lived or who was president of the United States. She could not keep the simple details of her daily life straight. Hospital specialists had written her off. Upon her discharge from the hospital, she was pronounced hopeless.

Then the doctor who visited my office was called to the woman's home. He looked beyond the acute symptoms and found that, far from being irreversibly senile, the woman was suffering from a grossly inadequate diet. Soon after he prescribed improved nutrition, the woman's condition changed dramatically. Her memory improved, and once again she was able to cope with the stresses of her daily life.

By focusing on the disease that led to her hospitalization, rather than the whole person, the doctors at the hospital neglected, or were ignorant of, the importance of her nutrition. They were *ready to give up* on a woman who later proved able to enjoy a full, normal life. I can think of no greater tragedy, but it is unfortunately not rare, under the disease-oriented approach which pervades our medical care system.

Proper nutrition is a strong weapon available to policymakers, consumers, and health providers to attack the appalling rise in medical costs. But the fight is personal.

No matter how well we educate people on what constitutes nutritional health, the ultimate responsibility for health remains with the individual. In the end, each individual must make his own decisions about what to eat, or what lifestyle to pursue.

As a member of the former Senate Select Committee

on Nutrition, I participated in an exciting and bold initiative in the field of diet and health. We held extensive hearings on the role of nutrition in the prevention of disease and published a report on "Dietary Goals for the United States." Its goals are not the complete word on nutrition, but they are an important beginning—a first step in the right direction.

By emphasizing individual responsibility for a healthy lifestyle and giving Americans some needed guidance in ways of improving eating habits, the Nutrition Committee has made a valuable contribution to our thinking about health.

At a Pittsburgh hearing I held in nutrition, a sixth-grade girl told how, after some basic nutrition education, she planned the school lunches for a week in an experiment with the school nutritionist. That is a good time to instill good eating habits.

From a policy standpoint, it has not been easy to get our ideas on diet and health accepted by the executive branch. But recently our determination has begun to bear fruit.

The Surgeon General issued a report in 1979 on Health Promotion and Disease Prevention, the first of its kind. He linked diet with obesity, cardiovascular disease, cancer, and general health. The report concluded that if Americans cut their intake of alcohol, fat, sugar, cholesterol, and salt, they could reduce their premature death rate by 20 to 35 percent in the next ten years. At the third annual Conference on Nutrition and the American Food System, the assistant agriculture secretary announced tentative USDA/HEW nutrition guidelines as a precursor to a national nutrition policy.

We have neglected the other side of our message which goes beyond improper diet: to stress greater intake of fresh fruit, vegetables, and fiber, and more exercise. Our goal is not to manipulate, but rather to motivate habits of good health.

Pollster Louis Harris addressed this problem when he recently commented, "Discoveries in medicine will continue to be made, and the public will become increasingly more knowledgeable about health matters. But the major breakthrough in medicine will be one that changes the minds and hearts of the public, that strips away the illusions of invulnerability and the false hopes for miracle cures . . . and which leads the public to deal responsibly with their own health and positive lifestyles."

One bright alternative is the corporate responsibility for employes in the fields of alcoholism and drug abuse, with a number of major firms reporting a favorable cost-effective ratio in productivity and lowered absenteeism as the result. Others are promoting exercise, on company time, or are underwriting health club memberships either in or out of the plant—but, so far this effort is limited. Tax incentives for proven exercise programs benefiting a greater number of employes would be a positive step forward.

Because I believe so strongly in preventive medicine and in the private sector responsibility for good health, I devoted a major part of my comprehensive health reform proposal (discussed earlier) to preventive measures.

HEALTH CARE'S FUTURE

A major Republican stance has always stressed the capability of the private sector, within the framework of competition, to achieve national goals in a better and more cost-efficient manner than government structures. Government should encourage this process and should provide only interim solutions for periods when the private sector is temporarily unable to meet the challenge.

However, in the health sector over the last twenty years, this theme has been played out in a most unusual manner. It has been marked by heavy reliance on government, which has pointed to rapid changes in the national image of our health needs (mostly of its own making) and exclaimed that competition was mostly missing from the private health care delivery system. However, there is increasing evidence that *the need for interim federal solutions has passed.*

Meeting this nation's health needs in the 1980s represents a new challenge and, for perhaps the first time, we are capable of having the full range of America's health service needs met by a private sector displaying significant and increasing competition.

Many find health care in America in dreadful shape, and probably getting worse. By all appearances, they think, the only way that health care can be rescued is by massive infusions of federal money and federal bureaucracies.

Apart from basic philosophical differences about solutions, it is easy to understand why this approach is wrong —its basic thrust takes no account of the tremendous progress of the last twenty years. It makes no effort to build upon further improvements likely to occur in the next few years.

The goal of providing each and every American with access to quality health care can probably be achieved within the next ten to fifteen years, but only if we concentrate on *stimulating the existing system* and are not deluded into thinking it can be done better with more money and more bureaucrats.

Am I alone in thinking the system works well, that it

has gotten significantly better in the last ten years, and that it should improve further in the next ten years? In 1978 the Robert Wood Johnson Foundation published a major survey by the University of Chicago on the attitudes of Americans in 1976 toward the health care they receive, and measured it against some of the traditional complaints about the "inadequacies" of health care delivery.

The results were stunning, upsetting many of the preconceived notions the "experts" have been trying to foist upon us. Eighty-eight percent of Americans surveyed who had seen a doctor within the previous 12 months were satisfied overall with the health care they received, and the same percentage indicated they had a regular source of care.

Improvement is still needed, but that is precisely the point. We should keep working to *improve,* rather than supplant, the system we have. Yet the danger is very real that Americans will believe the regulatory rhetoric rather than their own health care experiences: 61% of the same survey respondents thought there was a health care crisis in America, and 26% were uncertain—even though most of these same individuals thought their own care was satisfactory.

These important changes in quality and access to health care have occurred over the last 20 years because of legislation that Republicans proudly supported. There has been a rationale for the government to intervene because there have been needs that could not properly be met through the private sector. This is of course changing, and the private sector should be doing much more, and the government less, in the 1980s.

THE ENVIRONMENT
AIR, WATER & PUBLIC LANDS

By SENATOR MALCOLM WALLOP

Many vivid memories spring to mind when I recall my
first days as a United States Senator. Not all are warm
ones. After I left my ranch at Big Horn, Wyoming, for
the trip to Washington on a subzero January morning,
my car ran out of gas and I was forced to hitch a ride to
the airport in the back of a speeding pickup truck seated
on a hay bale. *I like to froze to death!* Not surprisingly,
I found that no Senate colleague had arrived in so earthy
a fashion. The experience added color both to my cheeks
and to the reputation of maverick environmentalist
rancher which the media had recently formed for me.

It was a reputation which worried many Conservatives
and warmed environmentalists, for in my eight years in
the Wyoming State Legislature, I had fought for legislation which protects the state's environmental quality
and brings some order to the rapid energy-related growth
we are experiencing. Shortly after my arrival in the
Senate, it was the environmentalists who were worried and
the Conservatives who were warmed. The former, I think,
should not have been worried, and the latter should never
have needed warming.

The perceptions of both groups seemed to change
with the very first bill considered by the Senate Committee on Environment and Public Works, the Clean Air

Act Amendments of 1977. It was no doubt the most complex and possibly the most important environment bill considered during my two year tenure on the committee.

Of the 25 roll call votes the committee cast on the bill, I voted often for state rather than federal control, recognition of vested property rights, the establishment of standards free of directives on how they were to be met, and against amendments designed to protect regional commercial interests rather than the environment. These votes, more often than not, were negative checks on the environmentalist's scorecard. Washington's environmental lobbyists were clearly miffed, and my mailbags were very full. I was charged with having changed my stripes.

The principles guiding my votes, both in the state legislature and the United States Senate were, I think, consistent. They are Conservative principles which serve well and will continue to serve well as we enter the decade of the '80s. These principles are not only useful in assessing our air and water, but our public land resources as well.

The clearest starting point is to bite the bullet and recognize we *do* have environmental problems which cannot responsibly be ignored. The time has clearly come when we must consider the adverse environmental consequences of our actions—and correct them. Until the last ten or fifteen years, the word "environment" was not a household word. We did not seriously consider any effects on the environment, and it seemed we didn't need to. Air and water had seemingly endless capabilities to dilute and absorb pollutants. But no more. We are now forced to accept the fact that we live in a world of limits. We must recognize that dilution alone will not solve our pollution problem. We must accept the fact that the use of our habitat has the potential for harming our neighbors, not only next door, but far away in other states. Just as surely as our "right to swing" stops short of another man's nose, our right to use our habitat has its limits.

The resiliency of nature to accept intrusions has been —and still is—amazing, but her limitations are physical and biological fact. The environmental laws and restrictions we now have are an outgrowth of nearly a decade of extended political debate. Often, that debate has been disjointed and even misdirected, and the law sometimes reflects it. Nonetheless, just as it is unlikely that nature's limits will expand, it is unrealistic to expect that at any point in the forseeable future our society will totally reverse its direction, abolish environmental controls, and reestablish the preexisting situation in which we were able to use the environment with little or no regulation. As tempting as it may seem, abolishing the Environmental Protection Agency or hanging the President's Council on Environmental Quality from the yardarms by their toes would in no way reverse the basic commitment the country has made to environmental quality.

One might reasonably ask, "Why, after thousands of years of getting along, has it suddenly become necessary to regulate air pollution, water pollution, solid waste, the reclamation of mine land, the production of chemicals, and Lord knows what else?" It is a good question. It can best be answered, I think, by way of an analogy which illustrates the "exponential" effects of introducing ever larger volumes of pollutants into any system, including the natural environment. Let's assume that we have a 1000-gallon water tank with a hole in the bottom, which will leak at the rate of 100 gallons per day. We pour one gallon of water into the tank on the first day, and every day thereafter we double the amount we pour into the tank. We pour in two gallons on the second day, four on

135

the third day, eight on the fourth day, and so on. The sixty-four gallons we pour into the tank on the seventh day will leak out just as fast as we pour them in. Only toward the end of the eighth day will we notice any accumulation whatsoever in the bottom of the tank. By noon on the eleventh day, the 1000-gallon tank will be overflowing.

The same thing has happened to the environment: for thousands of years, our use of the air and water to carry away pollutants was well within the environment's ability to absorb them. Just as we did not detect the tank beginning to fill until the afternoon of the eighth day, by the time we detected our environmental problem, it had achieved a momentum which only enormous efforts could bring under control.

We began to address environmental problems, and our efforts were indeed great in the 1970s. The questions of the '80s will be, How, where, and why must we *continue* to address those problems, and how can we reconcile them with other, equally serious problems? America's answers to these questions will vitally determine the condition of our natural environment and our public health. They will be even more critical to our society, the free enterprise system, and our federalism itself.

In approaching our resources, we must first and constantly remember that air, land, and water are not only objects to be preserved. They are also God-given resources *to be used* in furtherance of our human endeavors. In each watershed, airshed, and parcel of public land there are not only public, but also private rights to be guarded. There are rights to be protected regarding the use of resources for the production of food, fiber, energy, domestic comforts, and manufactured goods. These private rights are every bit as sacred to Americans as a family home or business, and must be similarly guarded and respected.

This is particularly true of water. Managing water has traditionally been the responsibility of the states. Eastern states have used a system of law based on the "riparian doctrine" derived from the Common Law of England. There the Crown owned the streams and held them in trust for public navigation and fishing. When the colonists arrived in America they brought the riparian system with them, for it was well suited to the humid climate and the abundance of water.

The basic concept of the riparian system is that the owners of land adjacent to streams—or "riparian" owners —have an equal right to use water so long as their use does not substantially reduce the quantity and quality of water available to downstream riparian owners. Each water user must consider the rights of all other users and, in times of shortage, theoretically, each user is required to cut back water use to the same extent.

In the early days, each owner was entitled to have the stream flow through his land in its natural condition, and only rights to use water for domestic supply and stock watering were recognized. This was necessary and effective then, because it ensured that mills and factories powered by water would have enough flow to operate. Mills and waterpowered factories no longer dot the landscape, and most Eastern states no longer require the maintenance of a natural flow, so long as downstream use of flow is not unreasonably interfered with.

In the American West, conditions were very different. It was a harsh setting in which, more often than not, there was insufficient water to go around. Often, streams lost water and dried up, the farther downstream they went.

The riparian system, born of surplus, would not work. In addition, water uses in the West were different. Water was needed for mining and later for irrigation. Often water had to be diverted and transported substantial distances away from the streams. In many cases it was totally consumed in the process.

The West needed a system which imparted certainty as to the amount of water available, and encouraged the maximum use of what little water there was. Without certainty of water, the effort to settle the West would not have been worth it, and the Great American Desert might yet stretch from Kansas City to San Francisco. And so, as early as 1855, the "prior appropriations" doctrine developed out of the California miners' rule of "first in time, first in right."

In contrast to the riparian doctrine, the prior appropriations doctrine allows the use of as much water as can be put to a "beneficial" use. Since water must continue to be put to beneficial use to retain the water right, waste is discouraged.

Under this doctrine, water rights are not equal: those first in time have priority over those who start later. The effect of the rule is that water shortages—instead of being borne by all users—fall entirely on those who last started to use water. This allows each potential new user to size up the remaining water in the stream and make an educated guess as to whether there is enough water left to justify making an investment. Many a bad guesser went broke.

No two states have identical water law systems, be they riparian, appropriative, or some combination of the two. Thus, the rights which people in various states depend upon for their livelihood are not susceptible to the broad paint job I have just given them. It is enough to recognize that there are property rights to be protected with respect to water quantity and water quality, and the parameters of these rights are defined in each state's water laws, laws which were developed to meet the diverse circumstances with which men had to struggle in settling this nation of ours. These rights will continue to change as each state's circumstances change. To sweep these laws and these rights aside would not only be to deny predictability and certainty (which is the prime function of any law), but to deny geography and history as well. *State control of water must be maintained,* and with it the recognition of the very real property rights in water.

Unfortunately, the regulatory scheme we have fashioned to protect water quality has the potential of conflicting with both property rights in water and the state water law systems which order them. The scheme is complex, but I will try to put it in a nutshell. We have established water quality standards for a variety of pollutants, based on the goal of making all of our streams "fishable and swimable." Often the standards fail to take into consideration whether the pollutant may occur naturally in a given stream, indeed whether God originally made the stream fishable or swimable. Sometimes, in our zeal, we forget that He made cloud bursts, thoroughly silting the runoff, and as a consequence we make "cleaner than nature" the mandate: the best technology available to control the end-of-pipe emissions from a number of differing categories of industry is determined and, with that available technology as a basis, an industry-wide "emission limitation" is set, whereby each individual plant must meet the limitation in its particular category, regardless of whether that limitation is necessary to meet the water

139

quality standard established for the stream into which the emissions will go. Cities and towns are subject to similar —though not identical—requirements.

Prior to 1977, each pipe end, or "point source" at which pollution entered a stream would be required to meet these emission limitations, including the end of each of millions of irrigation ditches. Sanity prevailed, and irrigation return flows, along with runoff from nonirrigated farm lands, are now considered along with mine land runoff to be so-called nonpoint pollution sources. There is no direct enforcement power which can be brought to bear against these sources, and that is probably a good thing. Rather, each state is expected to develop and attempt to implement "management practices" designed to reduce runoff. These may not be totally effective. We do not have the power to enforce them, and there is not enough money available to implement them fully, if we did. Nonetheless, they are far preferable to the regulatory overkill which would otherwise occur, with no better actual results.

Another portion of our regulatory scheme of 1977 controls activities which most of us would not normally associate with water pollution. The now infamous Section 404 requires a permit whenever "dredged or fill material" is placed into "navigable" waters. Simply put, it regulates putting dirt into almost any water body that flows or is bigger than a stock pond. This would of course include both stream channelization and the diking off of "wetlands," activities for which the section was really intended. But it also places the federal government in control of construction, on private lands, of dams, roads, levees, and erosion control projects. The standard applied is less than precise: whether the construction would be in the "public interest"!

As I see it, there are *three major problems* with our water pollution control scheme: 1) it establishes goals which may not be necessary or desirable, 2) it fails to consider that our society has other goals to be reconciled, and 3) its requirements are often rigid and fail to take into consideration the costs of controls compared to the benefits we might expect to derive from them.

The fact of the matter is that making all of America's rivers and streams fishable and swimable may *not* be in our national best interest if pursued to perfection. In many parts of the country, streams often will not be used for either fishing or swimming, because lakes and other nearby water bodies far surpass man's ability to improve the streams. We must take a realistic view of nature. She is seldom constant in her endowments, and our efforts to make her every stream alike will be fruitless—indeed unnatural.

Meeting the goals of the Clean Air Act Amendments, including those that are misbegotten, will frankly take more money than we can afford. The Environmental Protection Agency estimates the costs of meeting our goals for 1983 to be in excess of half a trillion dollars. *We must concentrate on the most cost-effective approaches* to water pollution control, or the entire program will collapse under its own weight. Unfortunately, the present law does not allow the cost-benefit situation to be considered when requiring pollution control at any given site. Balancing the effects of pollution with dollars is not an evil sellout of our environment. In the long run, it is essential if the environment is to be protected.

Blinders have their place, but not on the collective head of Congress when it enacts any law. It is a comment

141

on the increasing complexity of our society that, more often than not, our recent laws do not reconcile adequately the bundle of other, competing, and sometimes contradictory societal goals into which they are thrust. In many ways, water pollution goals conflict with our water use goals. Emission limitations may require that an industry, or town sewer plant, have *no discharge at all*. The maintenance of water quality standards, or Section 404 requests, may require that no additional water be diverted from a stream and used. These provisions may keep water clean, but they may fail to recognize water's property value, downstream rights, and the real need to use it.

Not long ago, to meet water quality standards, a town in my state was required to build a wastewater treatment facility which, in effect, consumed all the water, returning none to the stream. This solved the pollution problem, the stream dried up! However, a downstream rancher, who had been using the water to irrigate for years under a state permit, was left high and, you guessed it, dry. Our policies cannot be so insensitive as to ignore the farmer who prays on his knees that there will be enough water in his stream for him to irrigate, regardless of whether it it is slightly below standard. And one can scarcely make the case that aquatic life benefits by the ultimate purity of total consumption!

We must stretch water a third way. It must be used, it must be protected and, finally, it must be further developed. America's demand for water will grow, from 270 billion gallons per day in 1960 to an estimated total daily use in 1985 of almost 430 billion gallons. If we build more storage facilities, and if we use water more efficiently, we may have enough water to see us through the '80s. If we do not, we may see the population trends of the '70s reverse overnight. The Sunbelt states could shrivel as quickly as they blossomed, while the Northeastern states, which have abundant water, could witness surprising growth. Buffalo, New York, rather than Phoenix, could be where the action is.

Our water use is expanding because our economy is expanding. Consider these statistics: it takes more than 30,000 gallons' of water to produce a ton of steel, 200 gallons to make one pound of synthetic rubber, and 184,000 gallons for a ton of the paper this book is printed on. It takes 4,000 gallons to raise one pound of beef and 1,300 to grow one pound of cotton. The implications for continued industrial expansion in many areas of the country are ominous.

Though our consumption increases, the total supply available to us does not. In a real sense, we cannot create more water. We can and must store more water in reservoirs, and conserve water at every opportunity. Innovative programs such as cloud seeding could increase the available water in areas of otherwise short supply. That increase could be as much as 8% in the Colorado River Basin alone. New technology and innovative programs must be vigorously pursued in the 1980s.

The Colorado is now perhaps the most tightly stretched river in America. The lessons we are learning from it should not be ignored in planning for our other great river basins. Depending upon which assumptions we use, the River will not be able to keep pace with development starting in the early 1990s. On the other hand, it may last well into the 21st century. The assumptions do not take into account the vast amounts of water which may be necessary for the development of synthetic fuel plants in the Basin, which are a major part of the domestic energy policies we are now developing. The importance of these plants to our economy and security would be

143

immeasurable, should our supply of imported oil be cut off.

One synthetic liquid fuels plant, of the type now favored by the Department of Energy, would consume ten billion gallons of water per year. If the goals for synthetic fuels are to be met, we will need *almost twenty* of these plants. When we consider that water development projects have typically taken fifteen to twenty years to plan and build, we are confronted with the horrifying thought that we may have waited too long to develop additional storage.

Both our water and energy needs and supplies are, of course, based on many assumptions, some of which may not come to pass. But while we are hypothesizing, we should throw one final factor into the consideration. Projections on the amount of water supply which we now have and how long it is expected to last are based upon coverage river flows. This assumption may not be wise. More than 700 years ago, the Pueblo civilization of the Southwest reached its apex. The Indians had irrigated land and built cities, all based upon the flow of the Colorado River. In 1276 a great drought gripped the region and left behind the dry, empty, Pueblo cities we now see nestled under cliffs.

That drought lasted about 25 years. Today the Southwest relies on two main reservoirs on the Colorado River —Lakes Powell and Mead—to tide it over during times of drought. They hold a four-year reserve. It is food for thought.

America is also experiencing problems and conflicts with the air pollution clean-up effort and its effects on industrial growth. While most of the public controversy which surrounded the Clean Air Act Amendments of 1977 was focused on the debate over emission standards for automobiles, the far more significant aspects of the Amendments were the provisions controlling the construction of new stationary pollution sources: factories, mines, energy facilities, and the like. These amendments, for the first time, not only established limits on the amount of pollutants which each facility could pump into the air, but recognized certain proprietary rights in each air shed, much the same as proprietary rights to water use discussed earlier.

The law now requires states, under federal standards, to manage and "ration out" pollution rights, so long as a particular airshed does not exceed the maximum limit of pollutants allowed. If the airshed already exceeded the limit at the time the law was passed, or if it subsequently should reach that limit, the states may not allow the construction of a new pollution source until another source of equal pollution potential has either reduced its pollution or completely shut down.

We recognized that industries have a certain property right to use air, a right which is a valuable commodity, and which can be bought and sold. Just as importantly, Congress recognized that clean air is limited.

In a sense this is disconcerting—the buying and selling of the very air we breathe. Upon reflection, however, we see that it is entirely reasonable. Certain environmental standards must be established and maintained if the public health is to be protected. It is proper for government to set limits. But beyond that, the right to use our limited resources should be controlled by a system which provides certainty upon which to base economic decisions and freedom for the marketplace, and which allows the most economically advantageous use of the resource. The discouraging alternatives are either dirty air, or government decision-making as to what should be built and where.

Our air pollution strategy does recognize competing goals, and it does respect the requirement that the resource be available for use with some predictability. However, it suffers from many of the same problems which plague America's water pollution strategies, foremost of which are an inability to establish standards that are clearly necessary, and an inflexibility and a cost-benefit insensitivity which seemingly plague *all* complex regulatory schemes.

The air quality standard established for ozone has come under particularly heavy fire. The problem with ozone is that we are not sure exactly how it is formed. In addition to being produced by man, it is produced— we believe—by swamps and, to some extent, by virtually all vegetation. Levels of ozone exceeding the standard have been measured seventy-five miles off the coast of Virginia—presumably not from any factory. It therefore seems inequitable to prohibit the construction of a major new energy facility using the best air pollution control technology available on the grounds that it would cause a violation of the ozone standard, when at the same time a swamp up the coast is pumping out twice the amount of the very pollutant the energy facility would produce. This is not a hypothetical situation, it has happened. In the 1980s we simply must demand more accurate information upon which to base our standards. The consequences are too great to do otherwise.

The individual emission limitations we have established are at times harsh and inflexible. If a facility does not meet the standards, it may simply be shut down. In part this is due to regulatory inflexibility. We rely upon

146

regulation, because it is firm and certain, but it may also be unjust and unnecessary.

An alternative to the regulatory approach to air pollution that should be considered in the 1980s is simply to charge pollution "fees." For example, we could charge a uniform fee of 12 cents for the emission of one pound of sulphur into the air. This would induce industries to cut down on their sulphur emissions just to the point where removal costs equal the emission cost, or 12 cents per pound. Below that point it would be cheaper to remove the sulphur, beyond that point, it would be cheaper to pay the fee.

Industries that can control sulphur relatively cheaply will do so, rather than paying the fee, while industries with higher control costs will clean up less and pay more in the way of fees. This would decentralize environmental decision-making and reduce our total cleanup costs. The obvious problem is that we have no way of determining beforehand exactly how much will be paid, how much will be removed, and how much will clog the air. As our regulatory burden increases, as it surely will in the '80s, it is an idea which should not be totally discarded.

The problems of water and air pollution and use are significant when taken separately, but their synergistic effects may be the greatest of all. Therefore, once we have realized that these resources are to be *used as well as protected,* we must somehow rationalize and coordinate the layers upon layers of environmental laws and regulations at every level of government which seeks to protect a separate aspect of the resource. The 1970s have seen an "environmental law boom" which will have a far greater impact upon our country than all of the Great Society programs of the 1960s put together. The Clean

Air Act, the Clean Water Act, the Resource Conservation and Recovery Act, the Coastal Zone Management Act, the Powerplant and Industrial Fuel Use Act, the National Environmental Policy Act, the Federal Land Policy and Management Act, the Endangered Species Act, and numerous other environmental statutes all must be considered and complied with before anyone develops or expands the use of any public resource. The regulations under these acts are complicated and, in many cases, their requirements have not yet been firmly defined.

From the viewpoint of private enterprise, all of these regulatory requirements taken together represent tremendous change. Traditionally, control over basic questions of when, where, and what types of industrial development will occur were decisions made by private corporations for well-defined economic reasons. But many of those decisions have now been transferred to public agencies. Moreover, the decision-making responsibility has not been transferred to any single public agency, but has been factioned out among a host of separate federal, stage, and local bodies which more likely than not *fail to coordinate* their actions.

The biggest problem presented by this factionalization is the uncertainty created in the timing—and, thus, the economic justifications—of any new industrial venture. The extent of this problem has yet to be assessed. Its severity will depend both on how well government agencies coordinate their actions under existing authority and how fast private enterprise can learn to cope with the new requirements. One thing seems certain: to the extent we lay on new burdens and reduce the ability of businesses to plan the timing and nature of their activities, *we will drive small business out* of the field and thereby solidify the position of big businesses, which find themselves better able to cope with both the complexity of the requirements thrust upon them, and the uncertainty involved in a particular venture.

Our creation of an Energy Mobilization Board in 1979 addressed the right problem, but badly missed the mark. Congress stuck a band-aid on the open wound of lagging domestic energy production *without* treating an underlying disease which will produce untold numbers of similar wounds through every segment of our economy. The problems which argued for the creation of an Energy Mobilization Board are no less present and pestering for all other types of industrial development in America. A critical challenge in the 1980s will be to see if we can reconcile the regulatory overlaps and uncertainties threatening to strangle American industry.

As a senator, I am often approached by both energy and manufacturing executives who are finding it impossible to complete one facility or another because of regulatory delay. It is not that they fail to meet the environmental standards which Congress and the states have put down. More often, what forces them to utter despair is the uncertainty, delay, and rapid changeability of procedural requirements. They often tell me they can live with the red light of denial or the green light of approval but find that the prolonged yellow light of *uncertainty* is absolutely intolerable.

The principles which guide our use of air and water resources may also be applied, to some extent, to our lands. Theodore Roosevelt once said, "Every man holds his property subject to the general right of the community to regulate its use to whatever degree the public welfare may require it." That is true, limited by wise Consti-

149

tutional safeguards of our private rights. A corollary to that principle should also be noted.

"The government holds public lands in trust for the people. These lands must be managed with the goal of encouraging their best use, whether it be conservation, recreation, timbering, grazing, mining, or some combination of them. Government must respect the varying private rights to use most public lands, rights which are absolutely necessary to accomplishing the goal of making the best use."

National parks, wilderness areas, wildlife refuges, and other conservation units are truly "public" lands in which only limited private-use rights are necessary and desirable. The air and water resources in these areas are similarly limited. The waters are reserved to flow freely and unimpaired to preserve the lands in their natural state and foster and develop wildlife resources found there. The air is protected by the strictest of standards, which allow virtually no increase in the level of pollution which might already be found there. And, in most of these areas, the already stringent air quality standards may be rolled back if the view of these natural treasures, or visibility from them, has been impaired.

As we enter the '80s we should take a serious look at new and innovative ways of offering the protection which these public lands, or public values in any land, deserve. Traditionally, when the federal government decided that a particular parcel of land was worthy of protection, it simply bought it from private owners, or carved it out of other federal lands. However, it is becoming painfully clear that governments at any level *cannot afford to buy all* the lands which have public values to be preserved, nor would outright government ownership be appropriate in all cases. We must explore innovative ways of encouraging landowners—and all levels of government—to preserve these lands and values *without* absolute federal ownership. We must find less restrictive, less expensive, and more productive means. Through scenic easements or tax incentives, we may be able to preserve worthwhile public values, while at the same time protecting private property rights and encouraging the maximum production not inconsistent with the public values we seek to protect. We may find that these ideas would be good business, good for the taxpayer, and good public policy to boot!

But on most federal lands, such as those now managed by the Bureau of Land Management and the U.S. Forest Service, the land should not be considered "public," but rather communal. Such public lands should be managed to maximize their usefulness for this and future generations, to private individuals and the nation. Their ownership should be thought of as a virtual *bundle* of property rights. As with water resources, the value of these lands to private enterprises which have for many years depended upon them may not be ignored.

Over the years, Congress has passed a gaggle of laws in an attempt to create the best blend of public and private uses of our vast public lands. The Multiple-Use Sustained Yield Act, The Forest and Rangeland Renewable Resources Planning Act, and the National Forest Management Act all direct the Forest Service to manage our national forests on a multiple-use sustained yield basis. The Federal Land Policy and Management Act of 1976, commonly referred to as the BLM Organic Act, completely restructured the public land laws and gave the BLM far-reaching authority to manage public lands and resources for a variety of uses. It required public participation in land management decisions both system-wide and for individual public land units.

The BLM has been harshly criticized for its efforts—and lack thereof—in implementing the law. Much of the blame lies with the BLM, and much lies with Congress. In its zeal to provide a comprehensive management framework for public lands, Congress may have given both the BLM and the Forest Service too much to do, without clear priorities or directives. Congress must of course require that these lands be managed in an environmentally responsible way, and that areas of outstanding natural values be identified and protected. Beyond that, valid *private rights* to use these lands must not be forgotten. Grazing, timbering, and mineral exploration and development must be fostered. Moreover, *certainty* in these matters is critical if our national and local economies which depend on public resources are to survive.

A prime example of the impact of public policy on private property rights is the situation we are now experiencing in Wyoming with the Bureau of Land Management's handling of free-roaming horse populations on public lands. Forty-eight percent of the state and a full-sixty percent of its southwestern corner are owned by the federal government. While some of this federal land is protected in National Parks and Monuments, wilderness areas, and wildlife refuges, the vast majority is to be managed for "multiple use," which includes grazing, mining, and oil and gas production, as well as the maintenance of wildlife populations and other uses thought of as public in nature. Interspersed through these lands are unfenced private or deeded properties. The proportion of federal to private lands in the area makes it absolutely necessary that these public lands be used for their full resource potential if local economies are to flourish and the national needs are to be met.

The Wild Horse Act of 1971 protected the free roaming horses, but also required the federal government to maintain control of the animals. Since then, the herd has increased to nearly seven times its intended size. An estimated 10,000 are now roaming across Wyoming range lands, both public and private. The damage they have done to public and private land, forage, watershed, and wildlife habitats is in excess of a half million dollars. The herd is expected to increase by sixteen hundred this year alone. Yet the Bureau's target for herd "reduction" is below that number, and clearly inadequate.

These animals cannot be considered wildlife. Most were domestic animals or their progeny which were set free or escaped. Their population will not be controlled by hunting, as are the deer, elk, and antelope. They may only be managed by the federal government. Yet they compete for forage with the game we prize, and with sheep and cattle destined to be food on our tables, shirts on our back, and shoes on our feet. In ever increasing numbers they are winning the contest.

It is crucial that those with land management responsibilities understand the interdependence and interrelationships of ecosystems. Those who live on the land and those who study natural systems know that each form of life occupies a niche in the web of life, and that the laws of nature cannot operate in the absence of good land management. Westerners *cannot fathom* the notions of environmentalists who seem bent on protecting the rights of every coyote to the point of destroying the western livestock industry, or animal protectionists who fail to see that too many free-roaming horses will destroy the range they are overpopulating, ruining it for both livestock *and* wildlife. The romantic notion that in unspoiled nature wolves and lambs skip merrily through the forest together should exist only in fairy tales, but it has fostered illusions about the sanctity of certain wildlife species, making good resource management difficult.

Failures in public lands management can be attributed in part to lack of clear congressional directive, in part to a misinformed public, and too often to insensitive or unaccountable federal policy and officials. By and large, the individuals who manage our public lands *are* talented individuals dedicated to good land management.

But too often, just when individual civil servants begin to understand the local problems, they are transferred and their local expertise is lost. (Unfortunately, there are also a few civil servants who seem bent on operating fiefdoms, creating credibility problems for those who follow.)

Too often, policies emanate from Washington, D.C., which are unresponsive to local problems and conditions, or stretch the letter and intent of the law. No absentee landlord, including the federal government, can manage resources as efficiently and sensibly as one who is on the ground with firsthand knowledge of the issues. They must also have enough authority to constantly balance competing interests.

The problems of decision-making far off in Washington, D.C., were brought home to a rancher from San Juan County, Utah, when he sought to make his annual move of sheep from one area leased from the federal government to another, more suitable tract of land for spring lambing. He was told that the Washington office was in the process of "evaluating" the land, and the Bureau's policy was to deny access to it until the evaluation was completed. He was vocal at first, but then completely speechless when the bureaucrat suggested that he simply "delay his lambing for a month." This may be easy for the bureaucrat, but convincing the ewe would be difficult indeed!

We err if we do not recognize and protect natural values on our public lands. However, to view lands as either wilderness *or* multiple use, to be preserved as pristine *or* raped and ruined, is to view land management with blinders. *All* federal lands should be multiple use lands, and wilderness should neither be considered locked up nor managed that way. Wilderness provides valuable recreation, watershed, grazing, hunting, as well as scenic, educational, and other values. Complex though it may be to determine, each area of public land use may be deserving of a slightly different mix of public and private uses if we are to manage our lands in accordance with our goals. The need to know and appreciate local conditions argues persuasively for increased authority to make decisions farther down the chain of federal command, or through state or local control.

It may be that by narrowly focusing on our environment—the air, water, and land resources—we have somehow gone askew. Today, environmentalism has focused on the natural environment to the exclusion of all other facets of our total surroundings, which are important to our lives as well.

When Webster set about defining "environment" he described it not only as our natural surroundings but as the "aggregate of social and cultural conditions that influence the life of an individual or community—a fairly broad definition. We have, however, gradually come to think of environment in very narrow terms.

In short, we have provided mechanisms to protect the most important parts of natural environment from degradation. But what of our communities, schools, homes,

155

our economic system? What of our social and cultural activities, our way of life? Are these parts of our environment—which are under challenge and will not be protected by what has now become known as "environmental" legislation—not equally important?

In the 1980s we must not neglect, but improve *the laws we now have* to protect the natural environment. We must search for new and innovative ways to use and protect our resources, less costly means of saving resources and landscapes by more fully involving private parties, local and state governments, and industry. We must also begin to look at environmental quality in the broad sense. We must take up the new challenges and begin to look at the *total human environment* once again, or we will have no hope of saving it.

Our legacy has been handed down from generation to generation, and the challenge is not new. To quote Theodore Roosevelt once again, from a speech to Congress in 1907.

> To waste, to destroy, our natural resources, to skin and exhaust the land instead of using it so as to increase its usefulness, will result in undermining in the days of our children the very prosperity which we ought to by right hand down to them amplified and developed.

We will not meet this thrilling challenge by eliminating the uses of man. To do so would be to unwittingly place new, far less surmountable obstacles in our path.

How well we meet these challenges in the decade ahead will be judged not by us, but by the succeeding generations. They will either be here and be as possessed as we are of the values of environmental protection, free enterprise, and federalism, or they will have "cut and run." The wasteland of natural and human environments can be avoided—but only with vision.